STOP T...

HRIVING AFTER ... ABUSE

DR. PAMELA J. PINE

FEATURING: DR. BECK STANLEY BANDA, JOELLE CASTEIX,
KIM LAKIN CREGER, BETH DONAHUE, LAQUISHA HALL,
...MBRY HARRIS, CHRISTY HEISKALA, HEIDI HENYON, LIANNE HOFER,
...ANNE HOYER, FATMA IBRAHIM, DONNA JENSON, ANNIE KENNY,
MARTHA LAZO-MUÑOZ, STRONG OAK LEFEBVRE,
...ALICIA LIMTIACO, SYLVIE MANTI, AKEREI MARESALA-THOMSON,
...LERIE MEOLA, MARY JO ROSS, LAURA SHARON, CHRISTY YOUNG

STOP THE SILENCE®

THRIVING AFTER CHILD SEXUAL ABUSE

DR. PAMELA J. PINE

FEATURING: DR. BECK STANLEY BANDA, JOELLE CASTEIX,

KIM LAKIN CREGER, BETH DONAHUE, LAQUISHA HALL,

TAMBRY HARRIS, CHRISTY HEISKALA, HEIDI HENYON, LIANNE HOFER,

ANNE HOYER, FATMA IBRAHIM, DONNA JENSON, ANNIE KENNY,

MARTHA LAZO-MUÑOZ, STRONG OAK LEFEBVRE,

ALICIA LIMTIACO, SYLVIE MANTI, AKEREI MARESALA-THOMSON,

VALERIE MEOLA, MARY JO ROSS, LAURA SHARON, CHRISTY YOUNG

ENDORSEMENTS

"I applaud Dr. Pine, and the powerful authors and survivors involved with this tremendously healing book, who so courageously are lifting up the very important voices of survivors worldwide! The testimony of their experiences of trauma, victimization, *and resilience* are inspirational guides for all who have suffered from child sexual abuse, and for all who dedicate their careers to supporting survivors on their path of healing. I am heartened by the bravery of all the men and women who shared such important journeys in this book and am thankful for how the stories and tools they have offered will raise awareness, increase compassion, and amplify the critical work of preventing child sexual abuse and promoting the support and resources needed for adult survivors. I share my sincere gratitude for the wisdom and love shared in these pages, which will surely help so many others to heal and indeed thrive!"

~ **Sandi Capuano Morrison,** MA, Chief Executive Officer
IVAT- Institute on Violence, Abuse and Trauma - www.ivatcenters.org

"Eloquently written with tangible and practical strategies for healing, Stop the Silence: Thriving After Child Sexual Abuse is a must-read for survivors and those who serve them. Each of the chapters is penned by a different expert or survivor imparting lessons not just for surviving, but truly thriving after trauma."

~ **Angela Rose,** Founder & Executive Director,
Promoting Awareness | Victim Empowerment (PAVE) & Survivors.org

"Offering practical guidance and eloquent prose, Stop the Silence: Thriving After Child Sexual Abuse enables all of us to learn from those who have experienced the fearsome side of life and whose courage has lighted a path toward a better future."

~ **Victor Vieth,** Chief Program Officer for Education & Research,
Zero Abuse Project, https://www.zeroabuseproject.org/

"I'm very grateful to my friend Dr. Pamela J. Pine, who I've known for many years for asking me to review the book Stop the Silence® - Thriving After Child Sexual Abuse and to contribute an endorsement of it. The book is a collection of 23 stories written by survivors/thrivers of child sexual abuse (CSA). The kaleidoscope of stories features people from many different circumstances and life experiences, and who live in various countries. It will appeal to a broad group of people including survivors; still traumatized newcomers who are just finding themselves; certified, experienced professional health care workers; parents seeking to understand child abuse; other providers; and members of the public. They will all greatly benefit from reading this book.

Each of the 23 chapters is written by a different contributor who has experienced CSA of various types. The first part of each chapter is entitled My Story. Their stories often include their sexual abuses as a child. The second portion is called The Practice, essentially an essay about the type and experience of the author, how they were able to heal, and what they have to share with others to do so. Finally, each author's basic credentials are given along with contact information, social media profiles, and personal websites.

The young survivors' trauma, fear, and confusion are revealed as are the predators' beliefs that sexual contact with children is okay. Secret grooming and subsequent sexual assault make the child think it may be entirely their fault. The fear of the abuse becoming known to their community ensures the majority of children will not freely disclose, and their silence keeps some from survivors ever telling their story.

We learn that sharing one's story can help one heal. There are various ways to tell one's story, but it frequently involves seeking another person who is healing from similar experiences, and a big leap of faith. Many of the chapters in Stop the Silence® - Thriving After Child Sexual Abuse resolve in the good news that one's dedication to therapy can grow into a much more meaningful life.

This book can be a catalyst to suggesting to broken and lost survivors of child sexual abuse that it's okay to reveal one's painful youthful experiences and may promote a path to healing."

~ **Bill Murray,** Founder, Director, National Association of Adult Survivors of Child Abuse, http://www.naasca.org/

"A survivor once told me, 'It isn't on me for what happened, but it's on me to recover and be back on my feet.' In our 30 years of experience working with survivors in Taiwan, we have found that an important thing to let survivors know is that they are not alone. One way to let survivors know they are not alone is to let them share how they reframe their individual traumatic experiences into a force for change for society. This Stop the Silence® - Thriving After Child Sexual Abuse book gives important voice to many survivors' experiences and goes beyond by having those individuals help guide others through what they have learned."

～ **WANG, Yueh-hao,** CEO of the Garden of Hope Foundation, Taiwan.
If you want to learn more about the work of the Garden of Hope
Foundation, please visit: https://global.goh.org.tw/

"This book will give hope and strength to all survivors. It will help them to take that first step to healing by giving them permission to tell the truth. The women and men whose powerful stories fill these pages, speak their truth, and share intimate details of their own healing journeys. They take the hand of the reader, leading them gently down the path that leads to peace. While stories of child sexual abuse are hard to hear, this book lets us rejoice in the power of the human spirit to heal and holds out a loving hand to help others heal as well."

～ **Jan Goff LaFontaine,** Author of the award-winning book,
Women in Shadow and Light: Journeys From Abuse to Healing,
https://janlafontaine.com/

"As a healed survivor, I was pleasantly surprised at the array of stories shared by the diverse authors and how each story allows the reader to witness the innocence of a future survivor. Furthermore, the stories allow the reader to enter the brokenness and despair of a survivor and his/her loved ones. In the aftermath, as each individual rises from the ashes of despair, it's satisfying seeing that the survivors came out of the horrible ordeal, stronger and wiser."

～ **Carmen E. Rodríguez,** Survivor/Thriver

Stop the Silence®

Thriving After Child Sexual Abuse

©Copyright 2023 Dr. Pamela J. Pine

With the Institute on Violence, Abuse and Trauma

Published by Brave Healer Productions

Print ISBN: 978-1-954047-97-6

eBook ISBN: 978-1-954047-96-9

DEDICATION

This book is dedicated to so many:

- To the children who need protection, to the child victims, and to the possible billion or more survivors/thrivers of child sexual abuse (CSA) around the world who have endured so much and worked so hard to heal and help others.

- To my nuclear and extended family members who have supported me over the years of working to help prevent, treat, and mitigate CSA: Jeff Summers, Risa Pine, Maxim Pine, my sister Amy Pine, and my parents who instilled in me the belief that I could take on the world.

- To Sandi Capuano Morrison, CEO, IVAT, who has supported every bit of work that I've suggested we take on and supported me through the trials and tribulations of it, as well as to so many of my other colleagues working in this field.

- To Laura Di Franco, CEO of Brave Healer Productions (BraveHealer.com) and publisher of this book who, working with honesty, integrity, and skill, encouraged the writing of it and moves so many people to healing in so many truly wonderful ways.

- To other colleagues I work with regularly, like Jan Goff-LaFontaine (https://janlafontaine.com/), Akerei Maresala-Thomson (www.akthomsonltd.com, www.trustmyrivr.co.nz), Ward Schline, and so many more, who have done, and continue to do, such important work to bring awareness and address CSA healing.

- To supporters like Zoe Kopp of GRACE Cares, who generously helped support the involvement of writers presented in this book (zoe@gracecares.org, info@gracecares.org, www.gracecares.org, https://www.facebook.com/gracecaresvt, Instagram @gracecaresvt), and our other donors and supporters.

- To Robert Smith, a former CEO of an international health organization, who allowed me to march on with a vision under "his" roof, while I declared that this work was both needed and possible and that I could do it!

- And to Amanda S. Thompson and others like her who tell the truth. Connect with her on Twitter @BSP_003

The beautiful image on the cover of this book is a watercolor painting by Sinclair Stratton, entitled "Illusion." Thank you, Sinclair, for letting us use this gorgeous painting on the cover of our book. You, the reader, can learn more about her work through the following website: https://sinclairstrattonart.myshopify.com

The symbolism of the dragonfly is profound and perfect for the focus of this book.

"In almost every part of the world, the dragonfly symbolizes change, transformation, adaptability, and self-realization. The change that is often referred to has its source in mental and emotional maturity and understanding the deeper meaning of life.

The dragonfly's scurrying flight across water represents an act of going beyond what's on the surface and looking into the deeper implications and aspects of life. The dragonfly moves with elegance and grace. The dragonfly is iridescent both on its wings and body. Iridescence shows itself in different colors depending on the angle and how the light falls on it. The magical property of iridescence is also associated with the discovery of one's own abilities by unmasking the real self and removing the doubts one casts on his/her own sense of identity.

The dragonfly normally lives most of its life as a nymph or an immature. It flies only for a fraction of its life. This symbolizes and exemplifies the virtue of living in the moment and living life to the fullest. By living in the moment, you are aware of who you are, where you are, what you are doing, what you want, what you don't, and can make informed choices on a moment-to-moment basis. The eyes of the dragonfly symbolize the uninhibited vision of the mind and the ability to see beyond the limitations of the human self. Dragonflies can be a symbol of self that comes with maturity. They can symbolize going past self-created illusions that limit our growth and ability to change.

The dragonfly has been a symbol of happiness, new beginnings, and change for many centuries. The dragonfly means hope, change, and love."

https://dragonflytransitions.com/why-the-dragonfly/

FOREWORD

By Akerei Maresala-Thomson

Talofa Akerei Maresala-Thomson is my full name. I'm originally from Samoa. New Zealand is my adopted country. I'm a child sexual abuse survivor, suicide survivor, and former youth gang member who turned his life around, becoming a Senior Sergeant, community leader, and entrepreneur.

I met my colleague and friend Dr. Pamela J. Pine in 2017 at the Institute on Violence, Abuse and Trauma (IVAT) Summit. Her involvement in our work helped me start coming out of my shell. I was a very angry young person and blamed every white person, as, apparently, they were the problem for my community's issues. But within a year, we had a major grant that Pam wrote that brought critical programming to New Zealand. I got mentoring, coaching, and pastoral care from her and her associates at IVAT, and I was able to build resilience. These people were critical in my growth and my development. The connection helped build the skills I needed to help me and also help my family navigate everything that was going on. You can read about my background and growth in my chapter, Chapter 23.

Along the way, I realized that my story wasn't unique and that there were a lot of people telling a story like mine. I realized that we can all help each other. It's important we recognize that we cannot handle all this alone. We have to do it together. Everybody has a role to play in a person's life.

The perseverance, skills, and resilience to cope—that doesn't just pop out of nowhere. I say this because, sometimes, we, as mentors, coaches, and people who are providing pastoral care for people who are vulnerable, may not always see the light at the end of the tunnel.

For those of you who follow football and know the name Troy Polamalu, I remember him saying on a *60 Minutes* special that football was our meal ticket. I would like to refute that and say, "No, that is not our only option."

We're not just security. We're not just bouncers or security guards. We are scientists. We're entrepreneurs. We're businesspeople. We are more than just the status quo. And we need to recognize that and do something with that understanding.

Today, I'm the co-founder of MYRIVR, a social-good community app that connects users with nearly 8,000 health and social services around the country of New Zealand, and a program to encourage local entrepreneurship. Pamela Pine has now been to New Zealand three times to help us train our service providers and conduct comprehensive programming that involves the MYRIVR app. We continue to collaborate to bring critical programming to other parts of the world.

In the future, I look toward MYRIVR becoming the largest enabler of community services globally, connecting those with the support they need within their communities. I know my work, your work, and our work is not in vain. Our people move forward because of people like me and people like you, dear reader. This book is also a part of advancing all that.

On behalf of my family and my community, and my colleague Dr. Pamela J. Pine, I'd like to acknowledge and give you, the reader, a great big thank you for your interest, concern, commitment, and any work you do that embraces these ideas. Because without people like us, there wouldn't be people to help empower others to flourish—and no one to change the world. Fa'afetai.

CONTENT WARNING
AND DISCLAIMER

This book contains themes that some readers may find distressing, which include:

Grooming

Physical abuse

Sexual abuse

Rape

Assault

Incest

Violence

Alcoholism

Addiction

Mental health

Suicide

Self-harm

Reader discretion is advised.

This book offers health and healing information and is designed for educational purposes only. You should not rely on this information as a substitute for, nor does it replace professional medical or psychological advice, diagnosis, or treatment. If you have any concerns or questions about your mental, physical, or emotional health, you should always consult with a physician or other healthcare professional. Do not disregard, avoid, or delay obtaining medical or health-related advice from your healthcare professional because of something you may have read here. The use of any information provided in this book is solely at your own risk.

Developments in medical or psychological research may impact the health advice that appears here. No assurances can be given that the information contained in this book will always include the most relevant findings or developments with respect to the particular material.

Having said all that, know that the experts here have shared their tools, practices, and knowledge with you with a sincere and generous intent to assist you on your health and wellness journey. Please contact them with any questions you may have about the techniques or information they provided. They will be happy to assist you further!

TABLE OF CONTENTS

INTRODUCTION | i

CHAPTER ONE

WHEN ABUSE FEELS LIKE LOVE | 1
RECOGNIZING SIGNS AND ARRIVING AT *"ENOUGH"* AFTER BEING LURED

By Dr. Pamela J. Pine,
Public Health Specialist, Director, Stop the Silence®

CHAPTER 2

BECOMING A CONFIDENT CANVAS | 11
CREATING DURING THE HEALING JOURNEY

By LaQuisha Hall

CHAPTER 3

THE SURVIVOR COMMUNITY | 19
RELATIONSHIPS FOR HEALING

By Donna Jenson, Founder of Time To Tell

CHAPTER 4

CREATIVE EXPRESSION | 27
A PATH TO RELEASE FOR RELIEF
By Laura Sharon, MA, ACC, CDWF/CDTLF

CHAPTER 5

UNDEFEATED | 39
FROM WARRIOR TO PEACEMAKER
By Fatma Ibrahim, Consulting Director

CHAPTER 6

NEWTON'S LAW OF HEALING | 47
USING MOTION AND GRATITUDE TO CHANGE YOUR MINDSET
By Joelle Casteix

CHAPTER 7

BE STILL | 57
THE HEALING POWER OF THE PAUSE
By Annie Kenny, Certified Victim Advocate and Divorce Coach

CHAPTER 8

IT HAPPENED, WE BELIEVE YOU | 66
FIGHTING TO TELL MY STORY
By Mary Jo Ross

CHAPTER 9

KILLING THE MONSTER | 76
SILENCING THE VOICE OF SHAME AND GUILT
By Val Meola, Author, CSA Advocate

CHAPTER 10

RESILIENT | 85
THE TENACITY OF A LITTLE GIRL AND BECOMING AN ADULT THRIVER
By Kim Lakin Creger

CHAPTER 11

BECOMING VISIBLE | 96
COMING OUT OF THE FOG
By Strong Oak Lefebvre, Ko'asek Traditional Band of Abenaki, NH

CHAPTER 12

RELEARNING THE STAIRS | 104
A FINE LINE BETWEEN LOVE AND HATE
By Beth Donahue

CHAPTER 13

FREE TO SPEAK YOUR MIND | 113
FACE YOUR WORST MOMENTS WITH CONFIDENCE IN FIVE MINUTES
By Christy Heiskala, CA

CHAPTER 14

FROM VICTIM TO GODDESS | 121
AN EMBODIED PRACTICE FOR ULTIMATE CATHARSIS
By Christy Young

CHAPTER 15

THE RABBIT HOLE | 131
NAVIGATING AND SURVIVING CHILD SEXUAL ABUSE TRAUMA
By Anne Hoyer, Administrator of Legislative and Special Projects for the Maryland Secretary of State

CHAPTER 16

FINDING COURAGE | 139
FIGHTING TO SPEAK THE TRUTH
By Alicia A.G. Limtiaco, Esq.

CHAPTER 17

THE EMBODIED PATH TO TRUTH | 148
HEALING WITH MINDFUL, EMPOWERING QUESTIONS
By Tambry Harris, MA Psy., Cert. Coach and Spiritual Guide

CHAPTER 18

HEALING WITH COURAGE | 161
THE DETERMINATION THAT MADE
THE PERPETRATOR SURRENDER
By Dr. Stanley Beck Banda

CHAPTER 19

BREAKING THE CYCLE | 168
YOU DON'T HAVE TO SELL YOUR SOUL TO HAVE MONEY
By Heidi Henyon

CHAPTER 20

FORGIVENESS | 180
PREVENTING THEIR BEHAVIOR FROM
DESTROYING MY HEART
By Lianne Hofer, CMWC

CHAPTER 21

FROM BROKEN TO BEAUTY | 188
HOW TO SHOW UP, HEAL, AND THRIVE
By Martha Lazo-Muñoz

CHAPTER 22

EMBRACING THE SELVES | 195
LEARNING TO GROW FROM TRAUMA
By Sylvie Manti, Diploma Hum.Psych, Bsc(hons), MPhil.

CHAPTER 23

FROM ABUSED, TRAUMATIZED, IMMIGRANT CHILD TO POWERFUL MAN, COMMUNITY LEADER, AND ENTREPRENEUR | 202
TAKING A BROKEN CHILDHOOD AND BUILDING A LIFE FULFILLED
By Akerei Maresala-Thomson

INTRODUCTION

Whether you're a survivor of child sexual abuse (CSA) or not, this book will touch you, teach you, and encourage survivors and others to reach out, speak out, and get the help that's needed to recover and thrive. *Stop the Silence*® – *Thriving After Child Sexual Abuse* provides heartfelt and poignant stories of abuse, recovery, and resiliency from male and female survivors of CSA and their supporters. It is a continuation of a new public health focus I took on in the year 2000 as a result of information that came in my direction, initially from the Centers for Disease Control and Prevention (CDC).

In January 2000, I sat in my office at an organization in D.C. that focused on international health, my chosen field, when information from the CDC appeared on my computer screen, calling for research proposals on all types of interpersonal violence (IPV). I spent my career up to that point working on some of the world's toughest health issues around the globe.

I started reading about the focus on CSA, given that my sister, Amy Pine, had acquired a reputation as a therapist who worked successfully with survivors of CSA–and I read, and read, and read. I was never exposed in school (public health!) or work to the issue of CSA, despite the below!

> "Every year, millions of girls and boys around the world face sexual abuse and exploitation. Sexual violence occurs everywhere–in every country and across all segments of society. A child may be subjected to sexual abuse or exploitation at home, at school, or in their community. The widespread use of digital technologies can also put children at risk. Most often, abuse occurs at the hands of someone a child knows and trusts. At least 120 million girls under the age of 20– about 1 in 10 [worldwide]–have been forced to engage in sex or perform other sexual acts, although the actual figure is likely much higher. Roughly 90 percent of adolescent girls who report forced sex say that their first perpetrator was someone they knew, usually a boyfriend or a husband. But many victims of sexual violence, including

millions of boys, never tell anyone." (UNICEF, https://www.unicef.org/protection/sexual-violence-against-children, retrieved November 9, 2022)

CSA occurs when an adult, adolescent, or older child engages a child in sexual activity for which the child cannot give consent, is unprepared for developmentally, cannot comprehend, and/or an activity that violates the law or social taboos of society. It encompasses a long list of various types of activities, usually perpetrated by those closest to the child (most of whom, but far from all, are men, most often from their families), including voyeurism, inappropriate touching, showing or involving a child in pornography, insertion of objects, and rape. It often occurs from a grooming process and can occur in all kinds of circumstances–in the child's room, parents' room, bath time, classroom, locker room, alone or with others, etc.

General and formal reporting is low due to its behind-closed-doors nature, power differentials, success at making the victim and families feel afraid and ashamed, and, due to age, reduced or lack of understanding about what is happening. Even if a child reports the abuse, the shame, fear, lack of resources, or lack of understanding often prevent families from seeking help. Without proper intervention, the consequences of CSA often last through adulthood, affecting us all.

CSA results in a host of poor outcomes for children, the adults they become, and society at large. CSA severely affects our neurology, a broad spectrum of mental and physical health outcomes, life expectancy, and the monetary cost to companies and nations. Other childhood traumas (e.g., physical and psychological abuse, neglect, parent incarcerated, parental substance abuse, which are a part of the spectrum of Adverse Childhood Experiences, or ACEs, per Fellitti and Anda, see www.ACEsTooHigh.com) are also extremely damaging as well as multiplicative in terms of negative impact. In comparison to the problem, little is being done directly by providers or the public, in an individual or a coordinated manner–but needs to be, could be, and must be.

Early on in my involvement in CSA, I wondered, given the public health impact: how could it be that neither I nor any of my public health colleagues (I did ask) knew anything about–were not taught anything about–the issue, the numbers, the devastation, the outcomes for the children, adolescents, adults, families, communities, and societies around the world?

I was shocked, horrified, and could not stop, and focused first on awareness-raising and advocacy since no one wanted to talk to me. I realized that if we couldn't talk about this issue, it would be awfully hard to do something about it. I could clear a cocktail party in five minutes in those early days!

I started working under the banner Stop the Silence® in 2000. We have gone on over these 20 years to focus on an enormous array of awareness, education, and training programs, and since 2021, as a Department of the Institute on Violence, Abuse and Trauma (IVAT). This book continues our worldwide efforts to bring awareness, understanding, prevention, help, hope, and healing to all.

I hope this book helps you better understand the issue and the need, as well as find the compassion and wherewithal to join us in whatever way you can—in protecting your and others' children, supporting survivors to heal, and bringing change to society.

Pamela J. Pine, Ph.D., MPH

Director, Stop the Silence®–A Department of the Institute on Violence, Abuse and Trauma, https://www.ivatcenters.org/stop-the-silence

April 2023

CHAPTER ONE

WHEN ABUSE FEELS LIKE LOVE

RECOGNIZING SIGNS AND ARRIVING AT *"ENOUGH"* AFTER BEING LURED

Dr. Pamela J. Pine,
Public Health Specialist, Director, Stop the Silence®

MY STORY

Sometimes things are enough. They are just *enough*. They are just simply enough. But it takes time, effort, and understanding to arrive at that place after being lured, manipulated, and molested.

Padma, an Indian American beauty with light brown skin and long, dark hair, was born in the late 1990s and brought up in the heart of Los Angeles, near the beach, by parents from a "good" family who immigrated from Mumbai, India in the mid- 90s. This was right around the time that Bombay became Mumbai, named after Mumbadevi, the patron goddess of the Koli fisherfolk, a simple people who migrated to the Indian islands from present-day Gujarat. Outside of her family's food, their stricter cultural expectations socially, and her love of silk kurtas, Padma was an all-American girl. She was smart and empathetic, did well in school, and was industrious, taking on an after-school job working with underprivileged kids. She was social and knew lots of kids, and they knew her. She was wise beyond her years and a little withdrawn.

She was 14 years old when she met Malcolm. English by birth, ten years her senior, he was handsome, with dark hair and dark eyes, intelligent, charismatic, articulate, funny, engaging, alluring, and a Casanova—a storyteller by nature, and a good one at that.

The story of Padma and Malcolm started with a simple walk on the beach. The day was calm; the sun was shining, and the waves, accompanied and encouraged by the slightest warm breeze, were lapping at the shore, adding to the beauty and drawing anyone with any sensibility to the deep azure water. It was a place for the heart. Padma had gone out to take in the bluest of skies, water, and warm sand. It was early spring. Malcolm was there doing the same thing. She caught his eye. He meandered to her side. He smiled. She smiled back. They walked together. The walk and the time getting a snack went on for two and a half hours, with them relaying their brief life histories to each other.

"I come from a family with a handful of siblings," said Malcolm at one point.

"We're all kind of artsy. I'm a writer, and I sing with my guitar. Another is a painter, and another is a filmmaker. I've spent the last few years working on a novel loosely modeled after my family. I'm hoping it'll be published and turned into a screenplay. I want to be famous," he said with a bit of a smirk. Saying it out loud made him feel slightly embarrassed, thinking that the idea was somehow small and self-indulgent.

But Padma was intrigued. Being in L.A., after all, there was always talk about this kind of thing; her classmates were influenced by the idea and the call of fame. In Padma's case, this was further supported by the fact that one of her uncles was a producer in Bollywood and had acquired a good deal of notoriety—and connections—in Hollywood.

"I might be able to help you," Padma said, looking up at him. She told Malcolm about her family connections.

Malcolm lit up: "Would you like to read my work, Padma?"

"I would really like that," she said. He promised to send it along to her in an email.

They sat down to have a Coke at one of the fast-food stands along the beach and continued to talk. He glanced down at her young hands. She was wearing three rings, all 22-karat gold, two on her left hand and one on her right, all made in India.

"What do these rings mean to you?" asked Malcolm. She smiled, feeling special and "seen."

"This one," she said, pointing to the ring on her left ring finger that had her initials on it, "was a present from my mom and dad. This one," pointing to the one on her left pointer, "was passed on to me when my grandmother died," she said. "And this one, with the garnet, is my birthstone. I was born in January."

"They're beautiful," said Malcolm, and added, looking at her intently, but not too, "And so are you."

Now Padma was not sure of what to say or do, so she remained silent for the moment and looked down shyly.

Before their first chance meeting together ended–when Padma knew her family would be wondering where she was–Malcolm confided something very personal. He told her, in quiet tones, that he was a survivor of child sexual abuse and that others in his family were, as well. He shared this story with her, not in graphic detail, but the circumstances of how it happened: an alcoholic mom who herself was abused and who was neglectful, and her brother, also a victim of abuse as a child, who was his abuser. To this, Padma was not sure of what to say again, but "I'm so sorry."

Before parting, Malcolm shared this: "Everybody leaves me." "Why does everybody leave you?" asked Padma. "I exhaust them," he said.

For a third time that day, Padma didn't know what to make of this comment or what to say. As they walked on the beach, there was the barest of conversation between them until they parted. But Padma felt like she had already fallen in love with this person who she hardly knew, who was too old for her, out of her cultural heritage, and definitively someone who her parents would not be pleased with at all. But he was so different than anyone she'd ever met. He seemed so open, so vulnerable, and she liked that. No one had ever spoken to her in this way. She felt very special, indeed.

And so, it had begun with a story. And so, it continued. And so, it ultimately ended.

Over the next months, Padma continued to meet Malcolm on or near the beach. He showed up with presents (a small new gold ring, like a mini-wedding band for her left pinky, a box of chocolates), read her his sentient writings, and sang love songs playing his guitar while she hid it all from her family.

How can I tell them? she thought. There was absolutely no way into that conversation. No way to have it if it were entered into.

In private, she read his writings, commented on them, and continued to meet him clandestinely. Padma could not explain the feelings she was having. Her ears actually buzzed when she was around Malcolm; her heart felt engorged, while the feelings in her stomach seemed to tell her to beware–she was almost nauseous. It did not all go together.

On their fourth meeting, when Padma snuck out of the house after dusk, Malcolm put his arm around her and bent down for a kiss, which she returned. It was after that that Malcolm suggested they go skinny dipping under a partial moon. "It's dark," he said, "and no one is around anyway, and the water is so lovely." It would be fun!

Padma did not want to seem too young for him. She wanted to feel grown up and available. And it was on that beach, after their swim, that Malcolm made his move. Padma was 14, and all of a sudden, she was afraid of so much. She was afraid that she had made a mistake, that someone would find out, afraid that Malcolm would leave her.

At that point, their relationship changed–and Malcolm himself seemed to change.

"You will never meet anyone else like me, ever," he told Padma one day, with what seemed like a sneer, with cruelty in his eyes and tone of voice. Padma did not understand the change in him. He demanded she show up when he wanted. While he seemed so available to her emotions in those very early days, he then refused to have conversations about her concerns and mocked her desire to talk, calling her "weird" and "crazy." He demanded sex. She started feeling destabilized and off-kilter, and her fear seemed to mount. She began doubting herself and her thoughts became obsessive. She wondered: *Is there something I should be doing differently? What more can I do to make him happy?*

She recognized him as hugely talented, and she thought that perhaps if she just "hung in there," she could reach him. His truly extraordinary talents, intelligence, and desire to do well seemed to make it possible, perhaps likely, that she could eventually help him, and she really wanted to. She felt a deep and heartfelt connection. This inspired her; she began writing poetry and sharing it with him.

Padma followed through on connection possibilities for him and identified people for him to reach out to. His book was published six months after they met, to quite the fanfare. He pushed her to try to identify others who might be able to further his writing. She called her uncle in India to get more names: "Hello, Uncle. I am doing some writing, and I was wondering if there are people you think I should show my writing to in the U.S." He complied with names and contact information, which Padma passed on to Malcolm, and Malcolm used, noting that "a close associate gave me your name saying I had enormous talent, although they asked me not to identify them as they didn't want to appear burdensome." And it actually worked, more than once!

One night, standing by the ocean, Malcolm had been drinking before meeting up with Padma. At one point after she arrived, he turned to her and said, "I feel like I want to hurt you."

Widened eyes and the quickest silent gasp registered her shock, sorrow, and hurt all at once. While there were changes in the relationship, Padma was stunned and merely replied, "Oh. I-I don't want to hurt you." When she brought it up while walking near the water a month later to understand what was going on, he denied ever saying it. "I would never say something like that," he told her. Padma did not know how to think about this–she knew she wasn't crazy. She thought to herself: *Did he believe he never said that? Did he not remember saying it?* She had no idea.

Padma became more and more uncomfortable over the next months. Her sense of being both drawn to and repelled by him increased. She became scared of him, of what he might do or say. She began to draw away while still accommodating him in nearly every way she had been. As she did so, she began getting clandestine messages on her electronic devices, including ones with her past private conversations and actions mirrored back to her, and her friends began acting strangely, breaking ties with her. She covered up the video access on her devices, except when she was talking on one of the platforms, exceedingly aware of being watched and overheard—stalked when she was on them. She became hyperaware of everything she did and said, on and even off electronic platforms.

One good friend, finally, months after these messages began, told her, "All our friends have been receiving emails and texts on all different types of social media from someone we don't know. The person has been saying terrible things about you. They said you were coming on to older men and making a slut of yourself." Hushed, with head and eyes lowered, she added: "And teachers got wind of it, too." She let Padma know that the media seemed tailored to each particular person, focusing on their relationship with Padma and what was important to them. Padma was devastated and talked for a long time to her friend about what she was going through.

Padma was amazed that no one exposed to the information, except the one friend, had contacted her to ask for her input. They just went along with what they were told. Padma became more and more exhausted trying to deal with the toxicity, underhandedness, lies, and cruelty. She recognized how deeply sorry she was that Malcolm was abused and that the result of that had been so devastating–and she also, despite trying to reason herself out of it, still cared, but finally also realized she couldn't take any more.

One day, after a year, when Padma met Malcolm at "their spot," she told him: "I can't see you anymore." Malcolm's eyes changed. Padma would describe that look afterward as reptilian, but he said only: "You will be sorry. You will never meet anyone like me again. You know you were the one who came onto me."

Thereafter, for a long time, the clandestine electronic psychological abuse ramped up 10,000 percent. She could not get away. She needed the devices for school and her work with the kids, but every time she opened one of the devices, she got messages seemingly coming out of nowhere. Some were beautiful and complimentary; some were horrific or blatantly and grotesquely sexual. She tried to reach him, posting positive images he'd like; if she got it "right," she'd get a positive message back; if "wrong," she'd be punished. It went on and on. She shook and stopped sleeping through the night. She didn't know what to do. She pulled back from her involvements, friends, and even from school, feeling like she had no choice.

Padma began getting sick, physically and mentally. *How could I have become such a vulnerable mess who wasn't paying enough attention?* she thought. Her family was beside themselves, understanding nothing about what was happening. They took her to the best doctors, who said, "She is suffering from a near emotional breakdown," and they prescribed Ativan to calm her. Padma was still afraid to speak out, knowing she could never explain what happened to her family or friends and that things might get worse for her if she did. Her anxiety and fear nearly completely overtook her. While it was not something her family would've supported normally, when Padma asked, "Can I see a therapist?" they complied. One was found. She began working through the tangle of feelings.

Padma also began reading everything she could get her hands on to understand Malcolm's behavior and her own. Ultimately, she seemed to comprehend and work through her issues and began to heal, and she finally reached the point of "enough." It was a long time, nearly two years, but if she was being honest, it was far longer than that before she began to feel somewhat like herself.

By the time she graduated, four years after it had all begun, she still struggled some. It was also a long time before she truly stopped blaming herself for what happened (which Malcolm tried so hard to ensure), realizing, as the therapist had been telling her, that "adults are responsible for their actions, and a child is never responsible for the actions of an adult. Adults have every responsibility to address their behavior, and they are responsible for getting the help they need." She could not help him. *Enough.*

THE PRACTICE

I would like to present the focus of the practice under the umbrella of something I call: Fundamental Understanding and Major Management (as in Fee, Fi, Fo... FUMM).

First, the Fundamental understanding part: there are some things we need to know as individuals, families, and community members. Additional information about child sexual abuse (CSA) is in the Introduction to this book. Please read that. CSA, which occurs worldwide in huge numbers, profoundly impacts people's sense of self and their lives. Outcomes for the children, adolescent, and adult victims and survivors can be terrible, even catastrophic. In many, perhaps most cases, including Padma's, there are people who could've recognized the signs and symptoms and helped. Also, pertinent to the story above, while most of those who've been sexually abused do not go on to abuse others, it puts survivors of CSA at higher risk for being abusive in various ways. It would behoove us all to understand the overall subject and dynamic–it affects us all.

There's a lot to learn about CSA, and now, thankfully, there is a lot of information available. Let's use that information to understand, prevent, and treat it. Barring major campaigns in the U.S. and elsewhere (which are still needed), we all need to take responsibility for knowing and helping. In a nutshell, we need to understand: What CSA is; Who it happens to and how (e.g., the grooming process); Who the perpetrators are; What the often-severe impact is on survivors but also on their families and communities; How to protect our and our neighbors' children and get them the help they and others' need.

And now for the Major Management part. I believe it equally important to say: I have heard people state that it's the victim's fault or that they cannot understand how a person could possibly get themselves in Padma's position. Perhaps they would understand it more, given her age. Still, people of much greater experience have found themselves in a similar position to hers, and perhaps more often than not, as a result of someone else's traumatic childhood.

Let's manage how we truly address CSA (and other adverse childhood experiences, ACEs). Let's make sure that we not only educate ourselves, our children (in developmentally appropriate ways), and our families, but let's also take a more active role in educating and training others. If you're not in this field, how can you do that? Some of it is fairly simple. If you go to the pediatrician, internist, family doctor, or dentist or are involved with legal matters, schools, politics, or any other field that involves children or families, speak out. Ask: "Do you have a policy on child sexual abuse? And if they say, "No," ask them, "Why not?" and "How can I help you develop one?" Please join me. Let's all do our part.

Dr. Pamela J. Pine grew up in suburban New Jersey and has lived in semi-rural Maryland from the late 1980s after returning from nearly a decade working overseas. She has been an international public health, development, and communication professional since the late 1970s concentrating on enhancing the lives of the poor and otherwise underserved groups, and an artist. Pamela has worked throughout the world, from Latin America to Oceania, on some of the world's most difficult issues, including Hansen's Disease (leprosy), HIV, tropical diseases, and childhood immunization/survival programs. She speaks Arabic and French. Pamela is a professor of public health, international health consultant, and, since 2000, the Founder, former CEO, and now Director (as of 2021) of Stop the Silence®, when it became the Department of the Institute on Violence Abuse and Trauma (IVAT), focused on the comprehensive prevention, treatment, and mitigation of child sexual abuse (CSA) and other adverse childhood experiences (ACEs). She is an expert in CSA and trauma prevention/mitigation and is called upon regularly by many to provide authoritative input. She was honored in 2017 with a Lifetime Achievement Award in Advocacy from IVAT. Pamela is on the Board of the National Partnership to End Interpersonal Violence and on the Advisory Board of the Clinical and Counseling Psychology Review, Lahore, Pakistan. Pamela holds a Ph.D. from UMD, an MPH from Johns Hopkins Bloomberg School of Public Health, and a Master's in International Affairs from Ohio University. Given a childhood interest in art and ongoing training that has included Eastman School of Music and Cornell University, she continues to paint, sing, and write – she is a bestselling author. In her free time, Pamela spends time with family and friends, paints, gardens, travels, reads, and exercises.

Connect with her here:

Email: pamelap@ivatcenters.org

Websites:
https://ivatcenters.org/stop-the-silence
https://www.drpamelajpine.com
https://www.amazon.com/author/pamela.j.pine

Facebook:
https://www.facebook.com/DrPamelaJPine2
https://www.facebook.com/stopcsa
https://www.facebook.com/groups/nikkilove

LinkedIn:
https://www.linkedin.com/in/pamela-j-pine-3123b78/
https://www.linkedin.com/groups/1867777/

Instagram:
pamela.j.pine

Twitter:
@StopSilence_CSA

CHAPTER 2

BECOMING A CONFIDENT CANVAS

CREATING DURING THE HEALING JOURNEY

LaQuisha Hall

MY STORY

Experiencing domestic violence over a long body of years caused me to eventually curl into an arched form and break onto a shore of onlookers who were shocked. They weren't expecting me to break right at their feet. The shock of many turned into a silence that swept over me—I never again wanted myself, nor anyone else, to experience the fear and anxiety I did.

I broke on the shore.

Afterward, I was vulnerable. Seeking support from any place or person who offers it can be detrimental. I learned this at 14 when I thought a grown man had my best interest at heart. Two years of sexual abuse led to me carrying guilt and shame while arguing within myself: *You are old enough to say something!* Attempting to protect my family from being hurt yet again, I left home at 16 years old.

I broke on the shore.

My past abuse and trauma-ridden spirit were evident while I attended a North Carolina university as a freshman. I walked about the campus with a heaviness. I maintained a look of defeat: no smile, often scowling, and my shoulders hunched over as I may have appeared inches shorter than I was at 5'10". I always felt like someone was watching or talking about me, which caused me to be extremely defensive and sometimes snap at people, "What are you looking at?"

Young men on the campus would offer casual compliments, "I like your dress."

Words from the young men set me off into a frenzy, "What do you mean you like my dress? Why are you looking at my dress?"

Confused, they would turn away and potentially assume I was strange. Frankly, I was disgusted with myself and everyone around me. How dare the world be happy and free while I struggled daily to find my self-worth?

I stopped seeking anyone's attention—I wanted the entire world to leave me alone. Because the world kept moving, one day I decided it was time for me to stop moving. After putting on my favorite dress and writing discomforting notes, I swallowed over 100 pills.

I broke on the shore.

When I finally decided to take back the night, morning, and my life, I joined a local advocacy group, the catalyst to the sounds of the tide that would end my silence. I found hope, strength, and solidarity through a group of women who survived just as I had. We cleaned up what was swept under rugs and rebuilt the pieces of our lives we thought we hid from the world.

What an experience to actually engage in the conversations I didn't think anyone wanted to hear! The leader of this group was so encouraging as well.

"LaQuisha, this is a safe space, and your voice and story matters here. If you want to share, you can. If you don't want to share, please simply enjoy one of the snacks on the table."

I looked at the leader closely. Did she have a story like mine? Was she really interested in hearing about me? How would I truly know if the space was as *safe* as she claimed?

I tested the waters. I briefly described that I was sexually abused by a pastor, felt ostracized from many I loved, and frequently grappled with suicidal thoughts.

The volunteers in the group so intently listened, nodding their heads in agreement as if they had experienced pain like mine before.

I broke on the shore.

But this time, it was a powerful break. I was finally heard and seen. I started to believe I could trust again. Out of nowhere, I no longer felt alone as I watched the leaders and volunteers nod, understanding what it meant and took for me to survive.

This was a breakthrough that empowered me to rise like the wave I was destined to be. I became a wave that rushed onto the shores bringing attention to the beauty of the ocean, especially the night I competed in my first pageant.

During the Mrs. Christian International 2008 pageant, I was fully covered in a silk, champagne-colored conservative gown. I stood with one hand on my hip and awaited my on-stage interview question. Whatever I was asked, I would have to answer in front of the audience. I felt nervous yet at peace as I smiled and stood so confidently still.

The host jovially approached me, "LaQuisha, I'm going to ask you the first question."

So many potential questions flared through my mind. *If you could have dinner with anyone dead or alive, who would it be and why? How would you describe yourself? What's your favorite animal, color, food?*

The brown-skinned man with aging hair smiled and asked, "What's the hardest challenge you've had to overcome?"

Without thought, I blurted out my testimony. In a room full of Christians, with one hand still on my hip, I told them all that a pastor abused me. "However, I will not allow this to hold me back. I overcame it because I am standing here today."

Suddenly, silence. I believed I heard the lights above us humming but I knew that wasn't possible. I didn't see anyone move. It seemed no one spoke for too long even though it really may have been a few moments.

The stunned interviewer replied, "Wow. I'm so glad you are here today. Thank you for sharing your story." He then moved on to the next contestant after glancing back at me one more time.

In that moment, I was afraid that I had said something wrong, yet I simultaneously felt that I proclaimed through an effervescent flow that my life had purpose and meaning, that it was vast and meant to be enjoyed.

I believe the world needs to stop ignoring sexual abuse and considering it "taboo." As a result of the advocacy group and the Christian pageant allowing me to find and share my voice, I now passionately advocate for this important cause, which has also helped me continue healing. I share my story of abuse, prevention strategies and warnings, and how others can help. I have supported, volunteered for, and joined other organizations and even created and begun my own programs. I believe that by mentoring and increasing the self-esteem of our youth, they will gain the strength to speak out if they're ever harmed.

It's our duty to protect all children from sexual predators. I do not want any child to experience what I did. Children should feel safe and secure in their homes. I want to see the laws pertaining to child sexual abuse changed to better protect our children. Each state has laws guarding against sex abuse. Additionally, each state imposes its own statute of limitations for this crime. The statute of limitations is the time frame within which a claim against any party responsible for the harm must be filed. An individual's failure to bring a lawsuit within the applicable statute of limitations could mean being barred from pursuing that claim in the future. There should be no limitations on time in any state, as each survivor's journey is different. The vicious cycle of children being abused and electing a time frame in which they should pursue legal action must stop now.

It took a lot of work to reach a place of *purpose,* to know and understand that my life has meaning. I used to journal a lot in my youth in the floral-designed diaries with a plastic lock and key, except I never locked them. While journaling helped me to release my thoughts, feelings, and emotions, it wasn't a safe place to store and record such personal information. I once learned this when an adult found and read my diary. I left it on my bed, unlocked, as I went about my day with a locked-down heart. I was hard to reach—I preferred solitude as a teen. After my journal was found, I was punished for writing about suicide and writing about negative wishes I had for family members. It was after my journal was found that I stopped practicing a strategy that was helping me to overcome so much hardship. It wasn't until adulthood that I picked journaling up again, but this time I did it through creativity and optimism.

To become a *Confident Canvas,* you have to believe in yourself. I did not always. Through a lot of support, prayer, and positive internal self-talk, I came to a place of presenting myself to the world with my head held high and an authentic smile on my face. No more hiding behind the secrets. I'm an artist: mixed media, hand lettering, bible journaling, watercolor, acrylic painting, creative journaling, and other forms of art led to my feeling self-assured again. I designed and created the life I deserved to live, a life where I speak boldly unafraid, seek the beauty that lies around me, and cease to tolerate maltreatment as a people-pleasing approach.

I created the 5-Point Journaling system. Since 2016, I have practiced this same journaling strategy to reflect upon my faith and fond daily moments. In my youth, I kept documenting the hurt and pain of the abuse I experienced. I wanted something different; I wanted to leave a legacy behind for those who follow my lead. The 5-Point Journaling system focuses on the positivity, beauty, and divine essence that I am and you are! It helps you not only keep the positive in front of you, but it helps you also move in that direction. Let me show you how.

THE PRACTICE

WHAT IS THE 5-POINT JOURNALING STRATEGY?

SCRIPTURE

Our spiritual well-being can be a grounding force when writing about our day or preparing to face the day. If you haven't ever considered writing words from your personal faith-based text, this is one of the five points in this strategy. For example, I often use the Bible app to copy the verse of the day. Some pull spiritual cards and write the meaning of the cards. Regardless of what faith or spiritual practice you employ, feeding your soul with positive words daily contributes to spiritual confidence.

AFFIRMATION

An affirmation is a positive statement you can write, think and/or recite that helps you eliminate pessimistic ideas and accomplish your goals. Write a positive statement about yourself that'll help you to challenge and overcome self-sabotaging and negative thoughts. This is especially important for survivors who commonly blame themselves for the abuse they endured. What happened to you was not your fault—affirm that.

QUOTE

We can find ourselves inspired by so many people and often the encouraging words they say. Copy a quote that inspires you. I have Googled quotes by people who inspire me, or I save them on my phone to copy later as I come across them on social media, in books, etc. Remembering the encouraging words of inspirational figures is uplifting, especially when your mind attempts to travel back to dark places of the past.

GRATITUDE

It's essential to reflect upon what we're thankful for. Identify what you're grateful for, specific to the day you're journaling. List at least three to five or as many as you can. Try to avoid cliché gratitude lists (yes, we're grateful for food, shelter, and family, but maybe on this day, you heard the birds chirp outside your window, and that brightened your day. Be thankful for the birds too). Unfortunately, our minds tend to focus on the negative and blur the positive occurring in our lives. This reflection time will put the right things in focus.

PONDERING

To ponder means to think deeply about something. Write the details about a positive experience that happened in your day. To maintain or increase our confidence, we must remember not to rehash negative situations or adverse experiences.

CONCLUSION

I have written these five points consistently since 2018, and this has helped me on days when I feel low, especially to flip through the pages of old journals, to see and read all the beauty of the stickers, paintings, drawings, and writing I created. Please know that you should modify this to fit your needs: maybe you will only write three or four points. Maybe you'll change one of my points to another topic? Whatever you decide, the goal is to be consistent and positive in order to further your healing. Jump into your journal and get to writing now that you have five prompts!

Through my own journaling practice, I created this method to help me heal and maintain my hope. I also want to leave a legacy behind for those I love; I want my family to pick up my many filled journals and, after reading them, feel like they can go on. I want them to seek the good in every day. I want them to remember that after all I've been through, they can make it through hard experiences too. I want the work I started and continue as I heal on my journey to extend beyond me and create more *confident canvases* in others.

After teaching this practice to people across the globe, many collectively break many shores alongside me now. May my journaling practice, your healing journey, and the voices in this book flood the Earth with a swell of great expectations.

LaQuisha Hall is a force to be reckoned with. She dedicated her life to serving her community and has been recognized by great leaders, including President Barack Obama and others. She has won multiple state and national pageantry competitions, currently reigning as Mrs. Maryland International 2023, expanding her reach as she teaches and advocates internationally for domestic violence, sexual abuse, and suicide prevention. As an artist, LaQuisha educates international communities on various forms of art and leads the #RevealYourTeal and #RestoreYourRoyalty abuse prevention campaigns through her brand, Confident Canvas.

Formerly, LaQuisha served as the international spokesperson and a board member for Stop the Silence®: Stop Child Sexual Abuse alongside Dr. Pamela J. Pine. LaQuisha founded the SheRose Awards to offer abuse survivors a platform to share their stories. Beginning her skills in mentoring at age 16, she also spent hours locally and abroad mentoring via Queendom T.E.A. (The Etiquette Academy), committed to encouraging and teaching teen girls about personal safety, etiquette, and positive self-esteem. She is the award-nominated and best-selling author of the memoir, Unholy Communion, a self-esteem journal for young girls titled Positively Bodyful, and the co-author of more than ten additional books.

LaQuisha is a proud educator and coach, serving youth and teacher leaders in Baltimore City Public Schools for 20 years and winning Teacher of the Year in 2018. Her "walk on gold" philosophy teaches communities to step off familiar territory and do extraordinary things. Find LaQuisha online at ConfidentCanvas.com or on Instagram @ConfidentCanvas and @LaQuishaHall.

CHAPTER 3

THE SURVIVOR COMMUNITY

RELATIONSHIPS FOR HEALING

Donna Jenson, Founder of Time To Tell

MY STORY

My dad was big, six feet two inches tall. He weighed almost 200 pounds. He was bigger than my bed. From age eight to twelve years old, here's what happens.

Some nights when he gets home from drinking, he staggers into the kitchen and clanks around. Some nights when he gets home from drinking, he staggers to the bathroom and then crosses the hallway to the bedroom where he and my mom sleep. But some nights, after he leaves the bathroom, he comes down the hallway toward my bedroom.

I hear his footsteps coming closer and closer. Boom, Boom, Boom. I say to myself: *Please don't come in, please don't come in, please don't come in.* I hear the door to my room open. I hide my head under my pillow. He closes the door slowly. I lie as still as I possibly can. He walks over to my bed. I pretend to be asleep. He reaches down and yanks the covers off me. I try not to breathe. He crawls up my bed and pulls my jammies down to my knees. I make myself go limp. He turns me over.

I send my mind to go look out my window. I make my mind count stars in the sky. I count all the way to the moon.

Suddenly there's wetness all over my bottom. I'm screaming, but I don't make a sound. He crawls off me. He says, "You tell anyone, and I'll kill you."

He leaves. I lie there like a fist—a fist that took decades to open.

I know that's a lot to take in, dear reader. So, take a deep breath, and exhale longer than you inhale. And, again, inhale, exhale.

Here's the good news—I recovered and built a life worth living. I chose a path that brought me through many healing experiences and into many healing relationships. I found my voice and more to defy my father's threats. I tell every chance I get.

When I was born in 1947, conventional wisdom said incest was a one-in-a-million occurrence. Now we know that if you walk into a random room with 50 people, there'll likely be ten who survived childhood sexual abuse. We're everywhere, and we need to find each other.

For me, the physical abuse started in infancy, the sexual abuse from ages seven to twelve, and the psychological abuse continued until my father died when I was 46.

The second layer of the trauma was my mother's denial. In our tiny railroad apartment, sometimes I sat on the floor in my room, back against the side of my bed, grasping a pillow to my chest and crying quietly. Walking past my bedroom, my mother wouldn't say a word. She'd slowly close my bedroom door, turning the knob so the latch wouldn't make a sound.

The third layer of trauma was the backlash after I disclosed the incest to my paternal biological family when I was 33. They decided to believe my father, who claimed he couldn't remember ever doing such a thing. He didn't kill me, but he did obliterate my place in the family.

Harm happened to me within relationships. I came to understand it would need to be through relationships that the wounds would be healed. We need relationships. And relationships are the hardest to come by when the first, most important, life-sustaining ones you needed were from your abusive family. The relationships that were supposed to be like the padded bars they safely lock down on you before the roller coaster takes off, the extra blanket tucked all around you on a cold winter night, the band-aids on a scraped knee. They were supposed to be protectors, plain and simple, to help you keep walking further into the world, becoming your whole self.

We survivors of childhood sexual abuse were taught to be careful who you trust, or worse, that you can't trust anybody. Because when you were at your most vulnerable stage in life–childhood–the main characters were either harming you or ignoring the harm.

Around me were paternal uncles, aunties, and a veritable hawk of a grandmother. None noticed anything except Dad's drinking, which was out of control. Given all my mother put up with, they all called her Saint Dorothy. These were powerful lessons about relationships, about who I could and couldn't trust. But at the end of the day, little me survived despite them.

Here we are, millions of adults who grew ourselves up—up from and out of our harm and neglect. Many of us have done all kinds of things to recover from all that nasty shit. We've taken on therapy and peer counseling, meditation and prayer, exercise and yoga, education and occupation, artistic expression, and time spent in nature.

It's incredibly healing to be in healthy, mutually respectful relationships. It's in relationships where we were harmed and in relationships where we're restored. Believing that, I spent years building a family of choice filled with people who'd love me like my birth family could not. I'm not sure if I could've disclosed to my family–knowing full well they might abandon me–if I didn't have my family of choice to catch me when the boom was lowered with lightning speed.

Yet, fifteen years down my healing path, I had no relationships with survivors. The room would be too crowded with two of us in it. It was too painful to imagine being with another one of us.

Once I started owning my incest experience, the last thing I wanted was to be around others who'd had the same experience. It was all I could do to cope with the memory and pain of my harm. I had no slack, space, or free attention for anyone else's trauma. The shelf was full. No, the closet was filled to bursting in those early days when my spirit was standing behind me, pressing her shoulder into the center of my back, gently nudging me to come out, to stop being the only one I let know about the abuse.

I at least had enough awareness to know I needed to break the silence and stop holding the pain and memory deep inside. It was like, okay, I can try and do that but don't make me do any more than that. *My arms and heart aren't strong enough to hold more pain and memory than mine.* And there's another thing. It would be just too damn sad to have to know, to look and see another kid who was hurt that way: too much information, too much reality, too much to hold.

But I got over it in small steps. And where I finally landed was in the wide-open vista of being fully known and understood by sharing lived experiences with other survivors. This becomes an eye-opening, heart-rendering realization that *you are not alone.* That's beyond value.

I've experienced an incredible level of healing in relationships with other survivors. "Nay, Nay," you may say—as I once did. *Hard enough to cope with my pain, not interested in feeling the heat of others.* But, oh, what a payoff once I started. To be with others who know how bad it feels, the shame, the isolation. To finally belong in a world in which I thought I had no right to exist.

Having relationships with other survivors has been unique to my healing. I mean, we get it, you know? We get each other, and so we get gotten. We get understood, get seen. I was being seen big time, which is enormous because, as a survivor, I wasn't being seen when all the bad stuff was happening. And then abracadabra, drop yourself into a relationship with another survivor, and all those doors get opened, and those walls crumble. The room becomes illuminated with innate understanding, and you don't have to hardly say anything at all.

The operative point of view between survivors is:

I believe you

and

It wasn't your fault

This is a complete reversal of the doubt and disregard we typically receive from many non-survivors, not to mention our culture at large.

My first survivor friend, I'll call her Eve, was in my weekly writer's group from 1997 to 2009. This group was where I first started writing with others about the incest. Before that, I only wrote of it privately in my journals. Each time I read out loud to the group, I'd cry through my words. Fortunately, the group was amazingly accepting of me. I thought I was the group's only survivor and was glad of it. One survivor story was all I could handle.

Eve and I started going out to lunch after group to a funky little diner. One day leaving there, I got in my car. Eve tapped on the window, I thought for a second 'goodbye.' She pulled a tiny one-inch square of paper out of her jeans pocket, pushed it into my hand, and said, "You can read this if you want; you don't have to say anything about it." She jumped in her car and took off.

I sat behind my steering wheel and unfolded a letter-sized piece of paper. I don't remember what Eve wrote verbatim, but she was telling me she was a survivor, too. She was always so glad to hear me read in the group because she didn't feel so alone as she did almost all the time. I think I stopped breathing a little. I was stunned. And then, I felt a vein of gratitude grow inside me; it started in my gut and spread through my whole body. As soon as I got home, I called Eve to thank her. From that day on, we both wrote and read our stories about our harm and survival. Writing our stories, reading them aloud, and witnessing them is powerful medicine.

My life is enriched with a wide healthy web of connections to survivors. Those connections were made because one of us was *out,* known as a survivor.

Here's how one survivor friendship got started. I just finished meeting with a Board of Directors of a non-profit about consulting with them on their strategic plan. Their mission was to help abused children. I closed my presentation by saying, "Having been sexually abused as a child, it would be an honor to work for an organization doing this critical work."

Leaving the meeting, I walked past a pillar at the back of the room 50 feet away from the group. A woman stepped out from behind the pillar and introduced herself, saying, "Hi, my name is Jackie. I work for this organization. I'm a survivor, too, but they don't know that." Our eyes locked. I put my hand out; she took it, and I said, "Thanks for telling me. I'm sorry that happened to you. Want to meet for coffee later this week?" The upshot? I didn't get the job, and Jackie and I have been friends for decades, supporting each other, writing, co-leading, laughing, and dreaming together. None of this would have happened if we hadn't disclosed who we were to each other. I'm so grateful we did.

When I say a "healthy, mutually respectful relationship" (that's HMRR, so let's call it a Hummer!), I mean one where two people are kind to each other. We all know what it feels like when someone looks at us with kindness—a look empty of judgment and criticism. This is someone you look forward to seeing, talking to, and being with—someone you remember with fondness. It's warm and welcoming.

We don't feel that way about everyone we meet. That's humanly impossible. But when I sense that spark of warmth and recognition, I get an inner message: *Hey, I like what I see and feel when I'm with this person.* Then I move toward the spark, reach out, and test it out. Take the risk. The risk can feel enormous. *What if they don't like me back?* Or *What if they are untrustworthy?* Or *What if I'm wrong and they hurt me?*

I say, push past the doubts and fears and have an internal wager with your yearning: *What if they turn out to be fun and friendly?* All those doubts and fears are rooted in our abuse history. I say, climb up on that mountain of fear and take a leap. Because when you land next to an open and ready survivor, the payoff will be grand.

Let's break it down, this Hummer. It's a relationship where both people like and care about each other, where we're giving and receiving equal amounts of attention. It's laced with kindness and genuine curiosity for and about one another. And, if and when a conflict arises, you both feel free to address it, deal with it, resolve it, and move on. In a Hummer, you don't worry about someone being adamantly defensive. When you find someone you want to be friends with, *be* one. Show up, stay in touch, ask about their life, and tell them about yours.

THE PRACTICE

Let's say right now you have no survivor friends and are ready to try and find one. How many people in your life know you are a survivor? None? Three? Maybe your partner, a therapist, and a best friend? Let's start with none. Remember, to find survivors, you must be known as a survivor.

One practice that might be a worthy first step is mirror work. I'm a big believer in mirror work. All you need is a mirror in front of you. You sit there and look yourself in the eyes. Start slow, and say, "Hi," with a smile. The smile is very important. When you say "Hi," it's possible random thoughts will pop into your head, like, *This is silly.* Don't let that stop you.

Keep going. Smile and say, "Hi." Then up the ante. "Hi," smile, "I'm so proud of you." Watch out; your inner critic could get ignited and send up a message of negativity, *Yeah? What's to be proud of? You got nothin'!* Ignore the critic; keep going. "I'm so proud of you and how you've survived." Take a nice deep breath.

The first time I did mirror work, it was on and off for a year. Maybe not every day but often, into the mirror in my bedroom where I did my hair and eyeliner. It vastly bolstered my self-esteem. Self-esteem is a critical ingredient for relationship building. As one of my favorite poets, rupi kaur, says, "How you love yourself is how you teach others to love you."

Try this:

Create a list of all your Hummers and the people who look like they have the spark to be one. Pick one. Let's say their name is Alex. Go to your mirror, take a couple of deep breaths, look into your eyes and say, "Alex, I want to share with you that I am a survivor of _____." Pause and repeat. Then go see Alex.

The more I tell, the easier it gets. And what I didn't know when I started down this path was how many people would open up and tell me they were survivors, too. Once you have that truth established, it's time to discover if they might make a good Hummer. And then? Well, enjoy the ride!

In her early thirties, **Donna** began her healing journey from the trauma of childhood incest in 1980. Along that journey, she has embraced many healing therapies and artistic expressions. She came of age within the second wave of the women's liberation movement in the 1970s, helping to build three grassroots women's centers. Jenson is keenly aware of the healing aspect of activism–the empowerment of standing up for the social change of one's own issue. By 1998 she understood that breaking the silence surrounding childhood sexual abuse was essential in eradicating the epidemic. That led her to write and perform her one-woman show, *What She Knows.*

In 2008 she founded her non-profit project, *Time To Tell,* to spark stories from lives affected by incest and sexual abuse to be told and heard. Her book, *Healing My Life from Incest to Joy,* was published in 2017 by Levellers Press. She was the editor of the anthology *Survivors' Voices: Works of Resilience by Survivors of Childhood Sexual Abuse.* In 2021 she produced the documentary "Telling Is Healing," specifically geared toward strengthening the relationships between survivors and their allies.

Time To Tell's ongoing programs include four virtual writing circles and one-on-one writing sessions for survivors: the Shared Stories Project with curated submissions from survivors; Beneath the Soil: A collection of Works by Queer Survivors of Sexual Abuse; and Donna's quarterly blog. She offers Leadership Development Coaching to both seasoned and emerging survivor leaders to reach their goals and realize their visions. See all this and more on her website www.timetotell.org

Donna lives on a wooded hilltop in western Massachusetts with her husband, Chug. Her most joyous time is spent with her family of choice, her grandson and daughter, writing with survivors, and as many days at the beach as she can make happen.

CHAPTER 4

CREATIVE EXPRESSION
A PATH TO RELEASE FOR RELIEF

Laura Sharon, MA, ACC, CDWF/CDTLF

MY STORY

"I feel really small. I can't breathe. I don't know what is happening," I said aloud as I drew my knees to my chest, enveloped them in my arms, and dropped my chin to my chest. In an instant, I became a tight, tense, hard human ball of flesh and bones. My neck ached.

I feared what I'd see if I opened my eyes, but the blackness behind my eyelids wasn't safe either.

The monster was coming for me.

"Try to take a slow, deep breath, Laura," Wendi said.

My body started to shake.

"I want to kick," I said.

"Kick what?" Wendi asked.

"I don't know. Someone is on top of me, and I want to kick them. Hard."

"Take another breath," Wendi said.

The smell of end-of-the-day aftershave and Scotch Whiskey wafted past my nostrils.

I am so small.

Warm, wet tears stream down my cheeks.

• • •

As I drove home from that therapy appointment, flashes of my childhood bedroom popped into my mind's eye. The porcelain bunny rabbit with cold, red eyes that sat on top of the white dresser with gold trim stared at me. Pink, burgundy, and green flowers on the sateen bedspread reverberated from the heap atop the thick, blue pile carpet next to the bed. My blue blankie with the navy blue velvet trim was tightly tucked in on all sides of the twin bed. It looked impenetrable, though it wasn't.

Some images flashed for a second and were gone. Others lingered.

Now, what the hell do I do?

I opened the front door and headed straight for my room.

I need to lie down.

Within minutes, I was fast asleep.

• • •

It was still light outside when I awoke. Slowly, I realized where I was and what had happened.

I felt wiped out. The heaviness in my body was a force that couldn't be ignored. It was in me and all around me. I felt like a toxic waste dump. I could've stayed in that bed forever.

I have to get this shit out of me. I feel like I'm being poisoned.

I rolled over on my right side, opened the cupboard beneath the built-in bookcase in my bedroom, and took out a sketch pad and a box of pastels.

A large sunporch extended the length of the house where I rented a room. A bamboo shade gave the illusion of privacy for the small part of the porch I could access from my bedroom. Beyond the glass walls, the backyard was surrounded by trees. In that space, I had a twin bed, a rocking chair, and a floor lamp.

The sun warmed the space and provided lots of natural afternoon light.

I sat on the bed, leaned my back against the pillows held firm by the wall behind me, and opened the sketch pad to a blank page. I removed the lid of the box of pastels and the piece of foam that sat underneath and on top of the chalk.

What color do I want? Red. Start with red.

I pried the red stick of chalk out of its foam bed and drew a red line across the page. The next line was straight and black. It ran parallel to the red one. It started at the upper right corner of the page and ended at the bottom left. I felt a lot of force behind that one. If it could talk, it would say, "umpf."

I picked up the dark blue stick of chalk and drew coils of circles.

What's next?

I picked up the black again and drew a solid circle in the center of everything. Always black.

I touched the color with my pointer finger and began rubbing the black in a circular motion. It got darker and more evenly distributed on the page. I kept rubbing until the circle resembled an Onyx.

A ray of sun beamed through the glass, illuminating chalk dust floating in the air around me. I got up to get a damp towel so I could wipe my fingers clean between colors.

Next, I added more concentric circles in orange and yellow. Then a turquoise blue and pink fern-like shape. I finished with an eye that looked more like a small sun in the upper left-hand corner, surrounded by more coils of circles.

I named this picture, which no one but me would ever see, The Eye of the Storm.

And as I cleaned up, I noticed I could breathe a little easier. My body felt lighter.

• • •

The roller coaster ride that is healing from childhood trauma consumed me for years. Denial is fierce, persistent, relentless, and our greatest protection until the price of living in denial becomes too high or consequential.

A few years into my sobriety, I suffered from gastrointestinal issues and symptoms of Irritable Bowel Syndrome (IBS). I saw two doctors, both of whom wanted to give me Valium and send me on my way.

"I can't take that medication because I am in recovery," I said.

They would look at me and reply, "Well, that's all I can do to help you."

For the love of God, seriously?

I decided to give one more doctor a try. He was in a practice I knew other recovering people went to, and I called to make an appointment.

The doctor ordered medical tests like a sigmoidoscopy. All the tests came back okay.

"I think you might benefit from acupuncture, osteopathic manipulation therapy, and biofeedback," he offered, and I agreed to try that.

During one particular visit, the doctor stood behind my head as I lay on the table. I could feel his warm hands cradle my head and start to gently rock it back and forth. I started to cry and covered my face with my hands.

"Laura, what's going on?" he asked.

"I'm afraid you are going to hurt me," I replied.

"I'm not going to hurt you, but who did?"

• • •

Naming the unspeakable is essential for healing, yet finding, writing, and/or speaking the words we have buried so deep or kept secret for so long or never even knew were yearning to come forth, is no easy feat.

As I wrote in my book, *When I Lay My Hands On My Heart – Healing Through Words and Color,*

> "If I could unfold from the fetal position and start my morning routine, snippets of memories tumbled forth. They would continue to emerge when I was driving, riding my bike, talking to a friend, or trying to work. The fabric of my day-to-day life was soiled with intrusive pictures. I worked [hard] to deny what was happening, to not notice the images and words that were coming into my consciousness...[Until] I couldn't hold back any longer..."

At first, the words and phrases that came to me were: "the monster," "smothering," "I can't breathe," "shot full of holes," "tight, hard, rigid," "don't ever let anyone see," and "not enough, never enough."

I was 24 years old and awoke one morning to the realization that no matter what I did or who I tried to be, I was never good enough. I was bad and unlovable, and there was no escaping it.

I wrote the words swirling in my head:

Right behind the 'I love you'
The bottle kept us stuck.
Airtight.
Nowhere to turn.
Who can I trust?
Maybe I'll be skinny…
Not good enough.
Maybe I'll cut my hair…
Not good enough.
Maybe I'll fall in love…
(you call me a whore.)
Not good enough.
Maybe I'll be the Mom…
Not good enough.
Maybe I'll run away…
Not good enough.
Maybe I'll be somebody else…
Never good enough.
Maybe you were right…
I'm not good enough.
Right behind the 'I love you'
I can hear the pack of lies.
Sealed tight.
Nowhere to turn.
Who can I trust?

Maybe I'll start talking.
Maybe I'll see the truth.
Maybe I'll start believing
Even I can trust.
Maybe I'll get sober.
Maybe I'll tell the truth.
Maybe I'll feel the pain.
Maybe I am enough.
Right behind the 'I love you'
The door slammed shut.
Airtight.
Nowhere to turn.
Who can I trust?*
(*reprinted with permission)

Getting the words onto paper created possibilities. I felt lighter. I could breathe easier. The tension in my body released.

• • •

Once I started to release the relentless churn of intrusive thoughts by naming the words and pushing color around on paper, the panic attacks became less frequent. The night terrors subsided.

Ever so slowly, I could tolerate the time between doctors' appointments. I also accepted that healing would take time.

I needed safe ways to express myself—ways that did not involve self-harm.

And I needed to learn to trust that I could be by myself. As I wrote in *When I Lay My Hands On My Heart—Healing Through Words and Color,*

"Through the process, I learned that to heal, I had to explore all the areas where I had been wounded the most: love, vulnerability, trust, self-worth, shame, and my body. But to do that, I had to risk being hurt again. The only way out was through."

Writing poems and drawing was my path. For two years, I only shared this work with my therapist.

Eventually, I had them bound at a local print shop. They gave birth to my recovery story, comprised the puzzle pieces of my life, and served as evidence of all my hard work to save myself from the depths of despair.

The ten bound copies lived in a box in my closet for 30 years. Now and again, I would show one to a close friend or give a copy to someone who was struggling.

As time passed and the #metoo movement emerged, I thought about putting these works into the world. I grappled with the fact that shame was still part of my story, but I was not going to let it kill me, as it had so many others. I survived. I mattered. My story mattered.

And even though I was terrified, I published *When I Lay My Hands On My Heart—Healing Through Words and Color* in 2019.

The fear and feelings of vulnerability that followed landed me in bed for several days. I honored this as part of the process, as I had done so many times before. I trusted myself to handle whatever came next. Most importantly, I knew that by taking the works out of the closet and placing them into the sunlight, I could help someone else find the courage to save themselves.

THE PRACTICE

Before you begin, gather up the following supplies:

- ✓ Pad of unlined paper
- ✓ Pen/pencil
- ✓ Crayons, colored pencils or pens, paints, pastels

Note: There is no right or wrong way to do this practice, and there are no right or wrong supplies. If you don't own a sketch pad, I encourage you to get one. Any drugstore variety will do, or you can get one at an art supply store. I also would encourage you to get some writing instruments that are colored. Again, no right or wrong with these. Just pick something you feel comfortable using that doesn't cost too much.

1. Settle Yourself.

- Find a quiet, comfortable place to sit.

- Uncross your arms, legs, and ankles if possible. Put your feet flat on the floor and rest your arms in your lap.

- With eyes open, lower your gaze or even close them if you'd like.

- Allow yourself to relax and settle in.

- Bring your attention to your breathing. Where do you notice your breath—at the tip of your nostrils? In your lower belly? Your chest? How would you describe the quality of your breath? Is it smooth? Ragged? Tight?

- Keep focusing on your breath, and take one long, deep inhale and exhale through your nose. Go slowly as you breathe in and out.

- Take another one.

- And then one more.

- Repeat these three rounds of breathing until you notice yourself feeling a little calmer and more relaxed.

- Notice what thoughts come to mind.

2. Get Curious—Round 1

- Ask yourself, "What thoughts are going through my brain?"

- Write down your answer(s). Be honest. Don't censor yourself. Notice any judgmental voices that may show up (e.g., "this is stupid," "I can't do this," "I am not creative," and so on.)

- Write the words that come to mind on a piece of paper.

- Keep writing until you decide you are done.

3. Do another round of three deep breaths in and out through your nose.

4. Get Curious—Round 2

- Turn to a new, blank page.

- Open the container of the colored supplies.

- Ask yourself, "What colors go with the words I just wrote?"

- Pick up the first color that comes to mind. Again, just allow what comes to come. Don't censor yourself.

- Make a mark–any mark you want–on the paper. Again, notice any judgmental voices that may show up in your thoughts (e.g., "this is stupid," "I can't do this," "I don't know what I'm doing," "I am not creative," and so on.) Know that these judgy words are normal. Notice and name them as "judging," and keep going.

- What is the next color that comes to mind? Pick that one up and make whatever mark you want on the page.

- Let the colors and shapes come. Notice and name any judgy voices, and keep going.

- Do what you can with what you have, and when you've had enough, stop.

- Notice what words, thoughts, and feelings are present now.

- Write them down.

5. Do another round of three deep breaths in and out through your nose.

6. Get Curious – Round 3

- Ask yourself, "How do I want to express the thoughts and feelings that are coming up?" "What do I need/want to do to get these thoughts, words, and feelings out of my head?"

  ✓ Do you want to sing?
  ✓ Dance?
  ✓ Build a fort?
  ✓ Go for a walk?
  ✓ Chop wood?
  ✓ Build a sand castle?
  ✓ Cook a meal? Bake?
  ✓ Dig in the garden?
  ✓ Twirl around until you are dizzy?
  ✓ String beads?
  ✓ Play with Playdough or clay?
  ✓ Color in a coloring book?

- If all that comes up are hurtful thoughts—you want to harm yourself or someone else, or if nothing comes forth—try writing or coloring a description of it.

- And then notice how you feel once that is done.

Sometimes wounds related to creativity or creative expression emerge when we give ourselves permission to begin this exploration.

In a kindergarten art class, I finished my assignment, walked away from the easel, and declared aloud to the teacher, "I didn't do that very well." Those words—which the teacher sent home in my report card—spoke volumes about how I felt about myself at that tender age.

It's important to acknowledge your truth and keep trying. Giving up isn't an option. If you're unsure what works best for you, try different ways to express your thoughts and feelings until you find one that works for you. Stay curious. What works for you will come if you keep inviting it to come forward. And in the meantime, keep doing this practice of naming and writing words and putting color to paper; it will loosen the mortar of your bricks so you can begin to release for relief.

Laura Sharon is an executive and life coach, poet, author, facilitator, and management consultant. Working with Laura helps you become more calm, happy, content, and at peace with how you show up in life and at work. Laura—a believer in the resilience of the human spirit and an advocate for the transformative power of truth-telling and authenticity—uses a wholehearted approach to help her clients be their best selves. She has a way of asking wildly open-ended questions that help people get to the heart of what matters most and is especially passionate about working with mid- to executive-level clients. Helping clients grow their emotional intelligence and executive presence are Laura's superpowers.

Laura is a Certified Dare to Lead™ (CDTLF) and Certified Daring Way™ Facilitator (CDWF) and integrates Brené Brown's research into her work with clients, as appropriate. In addition to working with clients one-on-one, Laura offers Dare to Lead™, Daring Way™, Rising Strong™, and The Gifts of Imperfection™ retreats, groups, workshops, and presentations. Laura has a Master's degree in Health Education from the University of Maryland, is an EQ-I 2.0 Certified Practitioner, is trained in Positive Intelligence and the Mindful Schools curriculum, and has been a mindfulness practitioner for over 30 years.

Laura also is the author of *When I Lay My Hands on My Heart: Healing Through Words and Color,* a book of poetry and drawings that chronicles how she used creativity as a tool for healing childhood trauma. She is a contributing author of The Wellness Universe's two premier publications— *The Wellness Universe Guide to Complete Self-Care: 25 Tools for Stress Relief* and *The Wellness Universe Guide to Self-Care: 25 Tools for Happiness.* Laura's blogs and other stories can be found at https://blog.thewellnessuniverse.com/author/laura-sharon/ and https://medium.com/@laurasharon

Connect with Laura:

Websites:www.imperative-dimensions.com or www.laurasharon.com

Facebook: laura.sharon.3

Instagram: @laura.sharon.imperativedimen

Linkedin:
https://www.linkedin.com/in/laura-sharon-ma-acc-cdtlf-cdwf-7822468/

CHAPTER 5

UNDEFEATED

FROM WARRIOR TO PEACEMAKER

Fatma Ibrahim, Consulting Director

MY STORY

Back in 2019, I was watching what would be one of the small miracles of the universe, but it meant nothing. I was numb. The beautiful orange sun's hues melting on the majestic Nile river alongside the tree leaves did not ignite my usual awe or imagination; my loved ones became just names; I went through the motions in my work despite landing on a most exciting assignment. I was just pretending to be. Isn't this one of our superpowers, too? Many of us have become both Oscar and boxing championship material: having a charming smile that hides the fighting and pushing to the side of incredible inner chaos.

I thought this numbness was a temporary by-product of my thin willingness to live. Up until late 2018, I had zero recollection of my childhood sexual abuse (CSA). Nevertheless, the CSA left a deep imprint since I could ever make sense of the world. I had this continuous sense of emptiness, not belonging, and ongoing confusion. I could not recognize abuse even if it screamed at me, and I could not form deep relationships. I had a very limited range of emotions, trying hopelessly to understand how I should feel about situations with many mysterious and longstanding illnesses.

I continuously fought those states of being and became a master at achieving anything I set my mind on. To the outside world, I was successful: prestigious jobs (a lawyer in niche law firms before switching to development with the World Bank Group); solid multi-disciplinary education and diplomas; fluency in three languages; good track record in amateur acting, directing, and writing (which took me to different countries); 100-plus paintings; and blessed with friends from different walks of life across the globe.

These attempts to give my life value were far from enough. This pushed me toward a journey of self-discovery, where I started building a new foundation for myself with the help of amazing healers. I learned that I dissociate myself from my emotions as a way to cope, that I take on far too many responsibilities and that I do not see myself or my needs. Many interesting changes happened, and I became relatively more satisfied with life.

But then I hit a frustrating invisible wall, where I was constantly falling against a growing sense of anger and resentment, with setbacks in the health department. I still persevered and tried new ideas to deal with this poison. And probably because I was relatively more secure in myself, I started recovering some CSA memories, memories I had locked deep for 30-plus years.

Life started making sense, and I was excited to uncover the lining of this invisible wall (well, I thought I saw the entire wall back then!). I bought all books I could find on the topic, understood what I was getting myself into, and called on trusted friends to share the information.

Soldiering my way through things and not being in touch with the inner chaos inside, I didn't recognize that I had rejected life completely. That was also coupled with a close friend's betrayal (a classic theme for us survivors) and some family drama (genuine life and death situations), which were all beyond my "window of tolerance," as they call it in somatic experiencing.

I tried to re-ignite the spark, but I was numb toward everything. It was not the hysterical pain (that I'm adept at hiding from the outside world) where terminating my life seemed the only kind option. Paradoxically, just toying with the idea in those states would usually bring me back to life. I was in a different place altogether, where I was also numb to pain or the lack of it. My nightly habit at the end of those very busy days was to look at the bedroom ceiling for hours; *maybe this seeming state of resignation would give me some answers, inspiration, or hope.* But there was nothing. And with that, came the decision to end my life which I approached scientifically. I researched methods and decided what would work best.

To rehearse my way through the end, I visualized the process and reached the stage where my body was carried away. This was when a tiny voice screamed with revolt: *I will not be defeated.*

It was not a Hollywood moment where I danced in the rain with a renewed lease on life. Not at all. It was a moment of determination in the direction of life. It took me two years of struggle to stay alive, but that tiny precious voice kept me here. I tried every modality I came across. Some were very useful; some were a waste of time—but each brought me one step closer to where I wanted to be. In that journey:

- I had to relinquish my constant need to recover all the memories I buried (not easy for my Sherlock Holmes inclinations!).

- I learned that everything is stored in the body and that there are many ways of working with emotions and body sensations, far more important than constructing a story of who, what, how, why, and when. I learned that healing is about changing how I react to the past in the present moment, not about the story of how it happened (not to diminish those with a story who want to recount it; my path is just different).

- I understood we are all human. Not to excuse destructive behavior but to understand we're all perpetrators in different ways. No, I have not molested children, but being passive-aggressive, overly helpful to others, abruptly cutting relationships, or not recognizing my own needs is a form of being a criminal too. I know this is a tricky point. Oh, how much I hated the healers who pushed me to forgive! But we cannot be whole unless we accept ourselves and others. This is, in my book, different from forgiveness.

- I started to allow more feelings to come in; I learned how to deal with the constant disassociation. I stopped judging myself when I dissociated. I can appreciate how I resort to it when situations become too intense for my window of tolerance.

- I started to open up to people. I realized that I hadn't lived life despite all my grand achievements. I was just hiding from life through them. I'm now taking slow and small steps to be out there and live.

- I'm recognizing in increments that life is not about what's out there but what's in here. The only worthwhile achievement is to feel present and content in the moment.

- I'm taking more risks with my work and life. I don't need to be a zillion percent sure of myself before doing anything. Now, I can do things beyond my comfort zone (including writing this chapter).

Speaking of moving beyond the comfort zone, in early 2022, I established an advocacy and artistic platform on Facebook and YouTube on CSA's impact on adult women. I wanted to start this platform in late 2019 as an artistic project to scream about my pain and alert society of this undiagnosed cancer. The spark was a horrifying newspaper story about a child who was continuously molested by her uncle and ended-up dying of wounds her grandmother inflicted on her to protect the uncle. I know you'll be re-reading that last sentence many times because something is wrong with its construction. Unfortunately, the sentence is true. This is why I wanted to scream it out to the world. But then my mother was diagnosed with terminal ovarian cancer, and I had COVID, and long COVID, and had to postpone this project for quite some time. The project then morphed into something I appreciate more, following many iterations and discussions. It's now a platform that simplifies information on CSA's impact on adult women to help women understand why they feel this way and know that they're not alone. Available information in Arabic is scarce, and I wanted to share what I know with others who wouldn't have the same access to information. Art remains a component of this work, with a song and dance released and more to come. With more inner work, I want to still scream my pain, and also ignite hope.

Creating this page was not a walk in the park. I stopped posting after a while, and I was growing uncomfortable. It took me time to understand why. I'm not a therapist (and I make it very clear on the page), and I wanted only to share information that was relatable to me (I did not want to take responsibility for information I haven't lived, like marriage or children). All I needed was to say that I'm in the same boat without providing details, since I'm a private individual. To break out of that was terrifying. That night, when I decided to break the silence publicly, I filmed maybe nine videos and couldn't sleep. I felt stigmatized by the entire world and imagined being rejected by my family, fired from work, and many more dramatic thoughts. Nothing happened. I "survived" to write about it and share my practice with you.

THE PRACTICE

With everything I tried, I learned that gentleness is key. Remember, I always soldier my way through things. I always look for a solution. That's not bad in itself; pushing can be very beneficial when done at the right time. But overdoing it makes life unbearable; it's being in a constant state of fighting with self. Now my solution is not to look for a solution! And the key to this is to accept and make peace with whatever state you are in. In other words, learn to relax where you are. This way, you create space for things to reveal themselves or change and also create genuine inner strength. I know it sounds like rainbows and unicorns, but it's not. Sometimes, relaxing is accepting being in deep pain and not rushing to find a fix for it. When I started to recognize that I couldn't move forward except by relaxing, I gave it a go.

Before I take you through it, I want to assure you that I know this practice can sound insulting or nonsensical. This is how I felt about it when it was presented to me by different guides and books: *What does it mean to relax? And how can I relax? How can I not always be hypervigilant to protect myself from anything and everything? Would I make myself prey to the universe if I allowed myself to relax?*

I was always waiting for the other shoe to drop, and relaxing meant the entire universe would drop. Relaxing can be very scary. It's the antithesis of everything we've lived, known, and experienced. As convoluted as it may sound, we seek comfort in what we know even if it's pain, fear, and limitations. At least we know what to expect, and we can defend ourselves. But speak of the absence of parameters when we enter a new world not bound by fear, calculations, hypervigilance, and expectations of the worst. Sometimes, relaxing means relaxing in the face of your terror triggered by happiness. I know, another seemingly paradoxical statement but it's more common than we think. I'm still learning to navigate that world, but it does make a hell (or maybe heaven) of difference.

Learning to relax is a journey that can be achieved with others and alone. With others, you can learn to practice martial arts, yoga, meditation, somatic experiencing, and have massages—all of which I'm a huge advocate of because they build your resilience and teach you to befriend your body.

What I want to show you here is something you can do on your own, wherever and whenever you are. We face difficult emotions or obsessive thoughts many times during the day, including when we're with others. This is a muscle I invite you to build so you can practice it anywhere.

I will preface it by saying there is no one formula that works for everyone and that there are many variations of this exercise depending on where you are on your inner journey. I'll give you suggestions for many things you can do. Do not get discouraged if you end up even angrier when trying to relax (that is very normal, actually). Just take a break and try it again later.[1]

Step 1: Notice. We cannot relax if we don't see the emotions, thoughts, tension, and anxiety we're holding. We're so used to the discomfort that we're not seeing it. From my experience, the more I remove layers, the more I'm surprised about how I hold tension and discomfort in ways that are so normalized I don't feel it.

Step 2: Name it. Giving things a name helps us better deal with them. Just tell yourself, for example: *Okay, I'm holding tension in this area of my body; I'm having this bout of allergy because I don't feel comfortable,* or *I feel angry.* If you don't know how to name it, say, *"I'm uncomfortable."*

Step 3: Accept and acknowledge. Do not fight with whatever is happening. I know it's tricky. If we feel sad or in pain (whether emotionally or in our body), we want to change that feeling as soon as possible. Changing it means fighting with it and giving it more importance. This produces more tension. We can also fight those uncomfortable states through spiritual bypass or denying them by pretending we're over the feeling or the feeling does not even exist. This is

1 Particular credit goes to the teachings of Abraham Hicks (https://www.abraham-hicks.com/); Ayla (https://www.facebook.com/search/top/?q=ayla%20speaks) and Elias (http://www.eliasweb.org)

another form of fighting with self because then we pretend things that are happening are not happening – and no surprise we end up exploding. It's important to acknowledge that you feel like shit, in pain, unlucky, or whatever that feeling may be. If you want to give yourself the opposite message (such as in the method of fake it until you make it, which I use a lot), you can only do it successfully when you acknowledge that you feel whatever you're feeling first.

Step 4: Shift your attention. Rather than fight it, keep whatever you feel as it is. In some practices, you'll be told to sit with the feeling until it goes away because it ultimately does. I'm suggesting something different here so you can implement it in the middle of a work meeting, party, or whatever situation you're in. For example, you have neck tension. Acknowledge the tension, and then look for something else in your body that doesn't hurt. Direct your attention there or direct attention to something nice in the room.

Here are some tips to help you shift your attention

- Intentional breathing: I'm not talking about yogic breath, but just a simple breath to remind yourself and your body you're not in danger. Take a breath when you recognize a state of being you don't like.

- Find similar colors: Close your eyes, count to ten, and then open them. Try to find ten items of the same color once you open your eyes.

- Touch your body gently or kiss it: We have a history of loathing our bodies which has become part of who we are. We don't even know what it means to not loathe it. It's helpful to give ourselves and bodies a message of safety.

- Keep repeating as needed: Sometimes, we need to do this 50 times a day. When I'm in an obsessive mode (whether feelings or thoughts), I can repeat the color exercise five times in a row.

With this, I want to acknowledge your pain and remind you that you're not alone. Just surviving child sexual abuse does not mean actually living life. We all have that innate capacity to live life and enjoy its different hues. Thankfully, we're in a time and age where it's easier to break the silence and help each other find tools that can take us back into the richness of life. I love you.

Fatma is all about self-empowerment and simplifying knowledge. She started her career as a lawyer (corporate law and international arbitration), then moved to development with the World Bank Group, and is currently a consultant to many international organizations working on simplifying laws and regulations and promoting a culture of amicable dispute resolution. She is a mediator, restorative justice facilitator, and teaches mediation. She also films short videos on how to deal with emotions with the objective of simplifying the information and providing access to information as widely as she can. She is an artist in visual and performing arts. Fatma also established an advocacy and artistic platform focusing on the impact of child sexual abuse on adult women.

Connect with Fatma:

Facebook:
https://www.facebook.com/profile.php?id=100083221214065

Youtube:
https://www.youtube.com/channel/UCFksWullWB9W4mrYtKN0VYw

Linkedin:
https://www.linkedin.com/in/fatma-ibrahim-aa562710/

CHAPTER 6

NEWTON'S LAW OF HEALING

USING MOTION AND GRATITUDE TO CHANGE YOUR MINDSET

Joelle Casteix

MY STORY

"If you had only kept your legs together, you wouldn't be in this mess."

The woman sitting with me in our family room sneered as she said it. The ugliness of the words was polished by a veneer of perfect makeup and hair. Her hands picked at an errant string on the hem of her skirt.

They were the most hateful words I had ever heard.

"Did you hear me?" she asked as I blinked back tears.

I didn't respond. But she knew I heard. She wanted to make sure that if I remembered anything from that moment, it was that the fault was mine. The fault would always be mine.

"You *had* to have an affair with your teacher," she said when faced with my silence. "Now, you need to understand what you are."

To her, I was cheap. I was a slut. I was bad.

I was only seventeen years old. I just graduated from high school.

The woman across the room from me was my mother.

And her words caused me more damage than the preceding two years of childhood sexual abuse. It was damage that took years to mend.

Growing up in Southern California looked much better on the outside. We had a big, beautiful home in an old (by California standards, anyway) neighborhood lined with trees. My parents were "perfect." You know the type: Successful, good-looking, involved with the community. They had two daughters—my sister and I—and we were raised to "look the part." We were impeccably dressed, attended the right schools, belonged to the right clubs, and did what we could so that we were a reason for our mother to boast.

Inside the clean, white exterior of our house, life was quite different. My mother struggled with her mental health and spent a lifetime self-medicating with alcohol—alcohol that eventually killed her. She was the worst kind of mean: she knew I loved her more than anything and used that to hurt me.

My dad was a different story. Totally in denial, he loved my mother unabashedly and could not—or would not—see the damage she caused.

My sister and I did what we could. We survived, even when our mother did her best to make us enemies. But by the time I was in high school, my safety net was gone. My sister escaped and moved away to college. I was alone.

My Catholic high school, however, was my sanctuary. I was surrounded by kids and adults who told and showed me they loved me. My friends cared about what had happened to me. They listened when I screamed and held me when I cried.

By sophomore year, even the love of a peer group was not enough to save me. No matter how wonderful school was and how many people supported me, I always had to go home at the end of the day. One day, I couldn't do it anymore.

I didn't remember much from that night in 1986. But within 24 hours, I was in a psychiatric facility with burns on my neck. My father, in a panic, packed my mother up and took her to rehab.

I spent months in the hospital, but since this was the 1980s, little was done to help the psychiatric and emotional needs of teenagers. Branded "manipulative" by doctors (even though I was still suicidal), I finally went home. My mother completed treatment.

We went back to our perfect home in our perfect neighborhood. We never spoke of it again.

Junior year, I promised myself, was going to be different. Now it was time to prepare for college: my way out of the house. And I had what I thought was a golden ticket: I was a singer. Chosen to be a part of the elite touring choir at my high school the year before, I was encouraged to explore a music and performance career. Scholarships appeared. Universities wanted to talk to me.

Then it got better: a new choir director. Mr. H. was talented, young, and charismatic. Everyone loved him and wanted to be like him. He was bright, interesting, and funny. He demanded excellence from his musicians and related to each singer on a personal and musical level. He had all the traits necessary to inspire and excite high school kids. Being close to him meant that you had potential. You were *good*.

There was a problem. He was also a predator.

And from the moment we met, he knew I was the perfect target.

"Joelle," he told me in a soft voice that implied a quiet tension I had never encountered before, "I know about your struggles."

Embarrassed, I couldn't respond. *How did he know?*

He gave an understanding nod. "The school told me. They want me to look out for you." He saw my discomfort and invited me to sit down next to him. He put a hand on my knee.

"My dad was also an alcoholic," he said. "I know what it's like to feel so alone and so misunderstood that you want to die. If you ever need to talk, my door is open. No one understands like I do. Your secrets are safe with me."

I left the office flushed with gratitude. An adult had never been so open with me. He saw me—really *saw* me. He knew what my goals were. He knew my struggles. He would guide me. Mentor me. Help me.

I wanted all those things.

What I didn't want was to be sexually abused.

Mr. H began the process of predatory grooming immediately. In case you don't know, predatory grooming is how a predator uses lies, manipulation, threats, secrets, flattery, and other strategies to trick a child into believing sexual abuse is okay and natural. Grooming makes the child think the abuse is the child's fault, and it's the best way for a predator to make sure the child will seldom, if ever, disclose. I immediately fell into the trap.

Access was never a problem. Mr. H. always found time for us to be alone. It didn't take long for him to trick me into going to his home to "help him move." Alone and away from home and school, I was prey to his abuse.

Those moments are still an ugly blur, but I can tell you this: my body froze. In my mind, it was as if I was watching the abuse happen to someone else. As an adult, I know it was disassociation. At the time, it was simply my mind's way of protecting me.

I wasn't alone.

Mr. H. had special relationships with three or four different girls. It wasn't long before I learned that other girls also went to his home. But I pushed it aside. This—whatever this was—was not happening to other girls. No one else was confused and isolated. I willed myself to believe that no other girls lived in the growing hell that engulfed me.

Maybe another adult would help me. Maybe, just maybe, one of the adults who said she cared about me and prayed for me could be my key. She was a vice principal and a good Catholic. I was friends with her son. She was kind and understanding. *She would listen.* I gathered the nerve one morning and went to her office. I told her that something weird was going on with Mr. H. I cried and told her I didn't understand what was happening. But whatever it was, I knew I didn't like it.

She put a caring, mothering hand on my shoulder. At that moment, I thought she would act like I dreamed my mother would act—if my mother were kind.

"Joelle," she said, in a whispered tone, away from listening ears, "I already know. Mr. H. told me all about it."

Relief washed over me. *She's going to help me.* I sighed and let her lead me to a chair in her office. She sat beside me and put a hand on mine.

"It's okay," she said. "This is what it's like to be in love."

The walls of my life crashed down around me. *How could I have been so wrong?*

Love?

She wasn't done.

"You can't tell anyone else about this. No one will understand. Think about it: you could end up back in the psychiatric hospital for something like this."

The oxygen was sucked out of the room. I wanted to choke, but I was frozen in shame and trapped by fear. I held my breath as if I would never breathe again.

I was fifteen years old.

By the time I graduated high school, I was pregnant and had a sexually transmitted disease resulting from Mr. H.'s abuse. My peers, who found out about Mr. H. and what he did to me and other girls, blamed me. I had seduced him, they told me. I turned him into a predator. I was a baby killer for having an abortion.

"We don't care what happens to you," a former friend told me. "You did this. You destroyed everyone."

I spent my late teens and early twenties on my highway of self-destruction. It led me to dysfunctional relationships, a failed marriage, suicidal ideations, more crippling shame, promiscuity, self-sabotaging behaviors, isolation, and a life based on lies. It wasn't a life at all. My mother's words would not leave me. Maybe she was right.

Is it better to be dead?

Almost a decade after the abuse ended, I woke up and saw that I had to choose: I had to decide whether I was going to live or whether I was going to die. There wasn't much time—If I didn't change things, I would die. That much I knew.

Whether it was stubbornness or the fact that I didn't want the people who hurt me so much to win, I decided to live.

There was a problem. I didn't know how. So, I had to learn. And I did: with a little help from a long-dead physicist and his theory of motion.

Today, I'm in my fifties and thriving. I have a solid, twenty-year marriage and a teenage son who is vital, confident, compassionate, smart, and happy.

I've taken obstacles and turned them into opportunities—realizing that the biggest mark I can make on the world is to make sure that what happened to me never happens to another child.

In the past twenty years, I've written books, been a TEDx speaker, and traveled the world speaking out on behalf of other survivors. I've changed laws to help adult survivors of abuse, exposed abuse in institutions worldwide, and worked every day to outlast the pain and outwork the naysayers. I don't hear my mother anymore. I don't hear my former friends.

Don't be overwhelmed: I didn't do this all at once or overnight. While simple, what I'm going to show you is not easy. Time is your friend.

Your happiness is within your reach. You can flourish, and you don't have to do it alone.

THE PRACTICE

An object at rest remains at rest, and an object in motion remains in motion at a constant speed and in a straight line unless acted on by an unbalanced force.

~ Newton's First Law of Motion

Any motion, mental or physical—and no matter how small—has the power with habit to completely change your mindset. The most positive motion of all is the exercise of gratitude.

~ Newton's First Law of Motion, for healing the child sexual abuse survivor

There is nothing more discouraging to the survivor of child sexual abuse—especially a female survivor—than hearing about the morning rituals of the super successful. It's an unattainable goal: How can a person go through a dozen morning rituals for achievement when the hardest thing you do every day is simply try to get out of bed and pretend to smile?

Since we are on the topic of discouraging things, how about the people—both well-meaning and toxic—who have sat us down and said, "You need to snap out of it. Get yourself together." But no one shows you *how*.

When you're paralyzed by shame and in the physical pain of depression, how do you draw a map to healing?

Enter Isaac Newton.

Sir Isaac Newton was a seventeenth-century mathematician and physicist considered one of the most influential scientists of all time. He dealt with some seriously complicated stuff—but he figured out that if you boil the information down, the rules of the universe are quite simple. If you check out his First Law of Motion, you can see that he knew how to make very complicated information accessible:

"An object at rest remains at rest, and an object in motion remains in motion."

There are no complex formulas, no numbers to make your head spin. In fact, he doesn't even put a requirement on the speed of the motion. Let me say that again: *He didn't put a requirement on the speed of the motion.*

That's why we can adapt this law so easily into what I call Newton's Law of Motion for Healing:

"Any motion, mental or physical—and no matter how small—has the power with habit to completely change your mindset."

Now, we know that Newton never applied his Law of Motion to the healing of the survivor of child sexual abuse. But when we take that leap, the power and the potential are endless.

Human beings have three basic reactions to threats: fight, flight, or freeze. For survivors of child sexual abuse—especially those who were abused by an adult they loved and trusted, the typical reaction is "freeze." That's what happened to me. Not only did my body freeze, but my mind, heart, emotional development, ability to trust, and maturity froze. I became an "object at rest."

That freeze reflex had a friend. Shame, one of the top long-term effects of CSA, is also paralyzing. When wracked with shame, healing seems almost impossible. The object—in this case, me—would now stay at rest.

How could I break this mold? What could be the force that could change me from an object at rest to an object in healing motion? For me, it took a simple revelation: I had to move. It could be big or small—just as long as each day, I did *something*.

When I started my own process, even making a to-do list was overwhelming.

And then I remembered: Newton put no speed limit on his law of motion. All motion needs to get started is a little bit of force. So, I decided: *just one thing.* I can do just one thing. I can outlast my mother's words and my peers' scorn.

The first day, I made my bed (something I hadn't done in a long time). It was a minor miracle. On the second day, I went for a walk. I did a little writing on the third day—just a few sentences. These were things that before I would have easily put off to instead lay in bed or stayed frozen in shame.

Then, something happened. By the end of the week, I had moved forward more than I had in years. This wasn't about accomplishing anything but about moving and not letting the paralyzing shame win.

Soon, I stumbled on the goldmine: gratitude. For years, people told me about things I should be grateful for, but because the reasons weren't mine, gratitude felt hollow.

I had to make the gratitude my own. I started the same way I began my Newton's Law for Healing: in addition to doing something that forced me to move, I began writing down *one* thing every day that I was grateful for. The timing was important, too. If I did this in the morning right when I woke up (I keep a small notebook by the side of my bed), I found that my entire day was now anchored in that gratitude instead of shame.

The first few weeks of the gratitude entries were small: I was grateful for my warm bed. I was grateful for a good TV show. Finding things was a struggle.

Then, my ideas became bigger because my heart began to heal: I was grateful for a working car. I was grateful for my job.

The most amazing growth, however, began when I started to be grateful for myself: I was grateful for how I helped someone. I was grateful for the joy of my friendships. After a while, it was easy to write down three or four things every day. Especially after I began to spend one day a month going back and looking through everything I had been grateful for.

Then came the revelation: I was grateful for my *potential* as a human.

That was a turning point. It took me years of slow, deliberate motion, but it was there. I was really healing.

This process I began—Newton's Law for Healing—while simple, is not easy. You may struggle with finding gratitude or with taking one small motion each day. It may hurt. But remember: any discomfort you feel from this process shows that what you're doing counts. The pain of your life caused by sexual abuse was out of your control. Discomfort from changing your mindset to one of gratitude and healing motion shows you that what you're doing counts.

Incremental movement, no matter how small, is unstoppable. Gratitude is your engine.

Joelle Casteix is a journalist and leading global expert, author, and speaker addressing the issues that concern survivors of child sexual assault and institutional cover-up. With more than twenty years of strategic communications experience, Joelle is an expert in child sexual abuse prevention, healing, digital accountability, social media safety, and international online privacy issues.

Her bestselling publications include *The Well-Armored Child: A Parent's Guide to Preventing Child Sexual Abuse; The Compassionate Response: How to help and empower the adult victim of child sexual abuse;* and *The Power of Responsibility* (based on her wildly successful TEDx talk). Her award-winning podcasts include Deep Dive with Lauren and Joelle and The Unasked Podcast. Both are available anywhere you get your podcasts.

Joelle is most proud of her role as a mom.

You can learn more about Joelle at www.casteix.com, where you can find links to her books, podcasts, and publications.

CHAPTER 7

BE STILL

THE HEALING POWER OF THE PAUSE

Annie Kenny, Certified Victim Advocate and Divorce Coach

MY STORY

It was a normal day until it wasn't.

I sat in the trailer behind the church, surrounded by a group of wonderful women, in my second week of our Bible study group. My daughter Jane sends me a text.

"Can we talk when you get home?"

Ugh. I'm tired, and it'll be late, I thought.

"I'll call you on the way home," I reply.

"No, I need to talk to you in person," she insists.

When group ends, I quickly say goodbye to the other ladies and get in my car. I know something is wrong. I call Jane immediately; I'm starting to feel anxious. When she answers, the pain in her voice catches me off guard.

This was the day I learned that my husband was a pedophile.

"Whatever it is, we'll get through it together. There's nothing we can't survive. I have your back no matter what. Did you do something wrong?"

"No."

"Did someone hurt you?" Silence.

"Did something happen at school?"

"No."

"Did something happen with Daddy?" Silence.

"What baby, what is it? What happened? Please just tell me; I promise it will be okay."

Finally, softly she says, "Can I just send it to you?"

"Absolutely. Whatever you want to do. I love you so much. I'll be waiting."

I hang up the phone and wait for whatever text she is about to send me since she can't bring herself to say it out loud.

A few seconds or minutes or who knows how long later, I get my text message. It looks to be a picture of a man's bare feet. I lose my ability to breathe and pull into a parking lot to see what she's sent me. It's a video. I hit play. I see Charlie. My husband. He's in Jane's bathroom. My brain tries to catch up. I see her. I can't comprehend what's happening. For the next 90 seconds, I sit in the empty parking lot, alone and in the dark, watching.

And the Annie that existed yesterday shatters, disappearing forever.

I put the car back in drive and called Jane. I'm speaking fast now. I need to figure this out and take charge quickly.

"It's going to be fine. I'm on the way. I'll take care of everything."

"What are you going to do?"

"I'm going to make him leave. We have to call the police."

"No!" She panics. "I don't want to do that."

I calm her down and tell her we'll figure all of that out later and that I'm on the way.

"He keeps coming into my room and asking if I'm okay. I think he knows something."

"Get the video off your phone. Upload it to whatever it is that your phone backs up to. Delete it. Delete our messages."

We discuss options for her to be safe right now and realize there really aren't any. If she leaves, he'll be in the house alone with her little sisters. She tells me she'll be okay, pretending a little longer. Charlie texts me, "Are you okay?" I tell Jane I have to get off the phone and call Daddy, or he'll get suspicious.

He answers on the first ring. I jump right in.

"Hey honey, sorry, I'm running a few minutes behind. I got caught up talking to some of the ladies."

"Are you okay?"

"Yeah, just tired. But I'm on the way. I love you."

"Love you, too."

I'm shaking so hard my teeth are chattering. My brain won't work. I call my friend Angie. Just when I'm about to give up, she answers. I jump straight in and blurt it all out. I have her full attention.

"Annie, you have to call the police."

I don't know if I can do that. Jane doesn't want me to. And I don't know how to do that. How do I call the police on my husband?

She says lots of calm, logical things, trying to help me. She doesn't want me to go home and says it's not safe, but I know I have to. My children are there. We decide I'll call Charlie's best friend. Maybe he can meet me there.

I call Doug. He doesn't answer, but I leave a panicked voicemail. "Something's happened. Please call me back ASAP. On my phone, not Charlie's."

He calls back immediately. I just blurt it out; I'm running out of time. Doug doesn't hesitate and doesn't question the validity of the information I'm giving him about his best friend.

"Call the police."

"I can't. I just need to make sure he gets out of the house. Can you meet me there?"

"Yes, I'm on the way."

I call Angie back and tell her Doug's coming. We both feel safer. I'm getting closer to home. I don't understand. I think of Jane. Alone in her room. Waiting for me. I think about Charlie, and I feel sad for him. Knowing he's going to be arrested hurts me. *But Jane. Jane. Jane. He's a monster. We're calling him Daddy as we talk about this.* I feel sick but don't have time to pull over and throw up.

Doug calls me back. "I can't come," he says. "You have to call the police. I'll make it worse."

I hear what he's saying. I tell him I'll do it. But I'm lying. Because I'm right around the corner from home and out of time. If I don't show up within the next couple of minutes, he'll know something is wrong. I called Jane one last time.

"No matter what happens, do not come out of your room. But be listening. If things get out of hand, call 911. Don't hesitate."

As I pull into my driveway, I realize that no one knows I'm going home by myself. Angie thinks Doug is meeting me. Doug thinks I've called the police. I'm afraid, but out of time.

I walk up the side steps of our rambler and walk into the kitchen. I close the door behind me but stay close to it. My escape route. Charlie's standing there in the kitchen. He looks normal, like my husband.

"I know what you did," I tell him softly. "You have to leave. Now."

He stares back at me for a second. His face is still beautiful. "Okay," he says.

He turns and walks towards our bedroom. I feel relieved. Maybe he'll leave. He comes back seconds later, spitting nonsense from his mouth. Excuses. Words that don't make any sense.

"NO!" I say it loudly. He's startled. "Get out now!" He turns back towards the bedroom, this time more agitated. I keep my position by the door. Listen. He storms back into the kitchen. Quickly. Loudly. He's pissed now. I realize he has a gun in his hand.

"You want me gone?" he says. "Fine. I'll be gone."

He pushes past me and into the backyard. I follow him outside. It's too dark to see. *I hope he does it. Then it's over. Then whatever awfulness lies ahead can be skipped. No one will have to know.*

I go back inside and stand very still. Barely breathing. Listening. No gunshot. He's back inside within seconds. Even angrier now. He goes back into the bedroom again. My mind is racing. *How am I going to get him out?* I start threatening to call the police if he doesn't leave. I need some sort of leverage, some move I can make to stay in control and get him out. He's fake crying now about needing his daughters. I don't even hear his words.

"Get Out!"

"I need to say goodbye to my daughters."

"No! Please don't. Don't wake them up. Don't have them be a part of this. Just go."

My middle daughter, Lizzie, comes out of her room into the hallway. *Shit. How much as she heard?* He walks over to her. Kneels down. Hugs her. Tells her he loves her so much. I stay by the door. I need to draw him out of the house, not let him draw me into the house. No one knows to come. No one knows what is happening here. I tell Lizzie, "Go lay on Momma and Daddy's bed and turn on the TV, and I'll come to tuck you in in a few minutes." Charlie stands up and opens the door to the baby's room as I beg him not to. He comes back a second later. He kneels down by the door to put his shoes on, and I see the gun tucked into the back of his jeans. *He still has the gun on him! While he was hugging and kissing my babies. This is terrifying.* I just keep standing by the door. He stands up; I hand him his car keys and lock the door behind him.

I go into Jane's room. She's relieved to see me. I tell her how sorry I am. She tells me everything. Tells me that there's a video on Charlie's old phone that he keeps in the kitchen drawer. We go check, and the phone is there like nothing ever happened. I try to turn it on, but it's dead, so I plug it into the wall. As it powers up, we check and see if any videos have been deleted. It's clean. We leave the phone charging. We talk about calling the police.

"No. Please." She's exhausted.

"It's going to be okay. We'll figure it out." I promise. "Try to get some sleep."

The baby is still sleeping, thank goodness. Lizzie is awake. *What has she heard?* My phone won't stop going off. I finally answer one of Charlie's calls.

"I need my work clothes."

"I'll put them in a bag and put them outside the door. You can't come in."

I grab a bag and throw some of his things in it. I walk back out into the kitchen and over to the door, and I'm startled to see Charlie standing there at the door waiting for me. It's dark; I have all of the lights in the house turned off, so Lizzie will go to bed. *He must never have actually left.* I'm afraid, but I open the door to hand out his bag. He pushes the door into my body, moving me back, working his way into the kitchen. I'm pushing back as hard as I can, but I'm no match for him. He shoves me out of the way, runs past me to the counter, and grabs the phone that is charging. *No,*

No, No! My insides are screaming. I try to grab it. He's grabbing my arms, pushing me. It hurts, but I just keep moving. *I have to get that phone.* We are outside the doorway now, physically fighting over this phone. I hear whooshing in my ears. I don't know if we are saying words. I can't get my brain to figure out what's happening.

Finally, I yell, "I'm going to call the police if you don't stop!" and he loosens his grip for a second—a whiff of hope. I grab the phone with my left hand, push myself away from him with my right and get in the door and lock it behind me in one movement. My hands are shaking. My face is wet. I think I'm crying. *I love him. I don't understand.*

I call Doug back. He's insisting I have to call the police. *I'm not ready. I'm not strong enough. I love him. Jane is so ashamed. We don't want anyone to know. Can't he just leave and never come back?*

"You're being stupid," Doug says. "Charlie will never stay away. You and the girls belong to him. He'll never let you go."

I know his words are true. But I don't want to hear them, so I get off the phone and call Angie instead. She speaks logic. But I can't get to where she is. And then she says it.

"Annie, are you going to get a divorce?"

"Of course. I have to get a divorce."

"There's going to be a custody battle. He's going to fight you for the girls. If you don't report it, does it exist? Does it count?"

I realize my reluctance to hurt Charlie will hurt my daughters later.

I check on Lizzie. Still awake. I go into Jane's room. She's sleeping. I wake her up.

"I have to call the police."

"No. Please."

She doesn't want this to be real. I understand.

"The divorce," I say. "Your sisters."

Her face changes. She knows. She nods slightly as her eyes well up with tears.

"Please go lay in my room with Lizzie to make sure she doesn't come out and see the police."

She walks down the hallway, and I go sit in the dark playroom. Like I'm hiding. I look up the non-emergency number for the police station. It takes me through a gazillion different places before I get to a person. Then a police dispatcher. I tell the woman I need to speak to an officer and report a crime. We discuss specifics. She says an officer will be out soon. I go sit on a stool at my kitchen counter, across from the door and wait in the dark, staring. I just sit there in the dark for what feels like forever. I don't know what to do with myself. I just stare at the door.

Two police cars pull up, and I meet the officers at the door.

"Please be quiet. My daughters are sleeping."

The lights are still off; I don't know why I don't turn them back on. I tell the officers everything. They ask a gazillion questions. Walk around the house. Take pictures. Take Charlie's old phone. Have me email them the video from my phone. The older officer looks me straight in the eyes and tells me I've done the right thing. I feel like I've been holding my breath. I finally let it out. *The right thing. This is happening.* He tells me everything I need to do tomorrow to keep us safe. This is just the beginning.

I check on the girls; they're all asleep. I finally take off my work clothes and slide into sweatpants. I grab a blanket and the baby monitor and lay on the couch. I close my eyes. *Please, God, let me fall asleep.* But my mind won't stop. It keeps thinking. Replaying. I see a red flag. Then another. And another. And before I know it, I've pieced together years of them. I hate myself. I open my eyes. Maybe I'll stop seeing it all if I keep my eyes open. I pray: *God, please, please, just let me fall asleep.* I wonder if he's outside. Watching. I want to be asleep. Or dead. Whatever would make this fire of pain stop burning inside me. I lay on the couch in the dark, staring. I hear the baby.

"Momma. Momma!"

I go scoop her up and bring her out onto the couch with me. We lay down. She knows I'm not okay. She pets my face, one hand on each cheek, holding my face close to hers. I force myself not to cry. I just swallow it back down to the point that I'm trembling. This is the start of the division of myself, the two separate Me's—the one that looks normal on the outside and the one that is in agony on the inside. My sweet baby falls back asleep, and I keep laying there, watching the sky slowly shift colors into morning, and eventually fall asleep.

THE PRACTICE

Looking back on that first night, I have a hard time wrapping my head around where I am today. The days, weeks, and months afterward were filled with so much trauma, fear, and confusion. As I navigated the roller coaster, the one phrase I kept going back to over and over again was, "Be Still." It was the only way to settle myself and survive another day. Instead of reacting to each hit, I slowly shifted into a trust in a higher power and purpose. For me, it's God. For others, it might be the universe. The important thing was the acceptance that so much of this journey was beyond me and out of my control.

That faith and steadiness didn't just show up one day. It can take months of retraining your mind. You can start slowly. Give yourself a timeframe in which to process before reacting. So, when you get a text from someone triggering, or you find out that your plan isn't going to proceed as hoped, maybe start by making yourself wait an hour before responding. Then work your way up to giving yourself half a day. Or three days. Or whatever you can manage. If you have someone close to you that can support you and hold you accountable, maybe they can help you make and stick to your target time frame. Don't respond to your crisis until after you've been able to talk it through with your person. Or until after you've gone to your next therapy appointment.

This practice didn't just help calm my steps and get me and my family to where we were going. This practice eventually started to heal me. Instead of each hit or fall ripping me apart, filling me with devastation or confusion, I started to feel them less and less. Because I didn't have to figure it out right that second. I didn't have to decide what to do or process the entirety of the situation immediately. The grace to be able to not pick each problem up right away and carry it on my shoulders allowed me to stay standing instead of burying myself under each bad day. There is freedom in accepting that you don't have to have it all figured out today to be able to get to where you are going tomorrow.

Annie Kenny is a Certified High Conflict Divorce Coach and Victim/Child Safety Advocate. Her organization, Bloom Consulting, is dedicated to helping protective parents with their own personal family court battles, as well as promoting family court legislative reform. She is a member of her local Family Violence Coordinating Council, was a speaker at the 2022 Battered Women's Custody Conference, and has served as a panelist on the "Allen v Farrow" panel series. Her personal story has been featured by WJLA, and her family court Op-Ed was published by the Washington Post. She has collaborated with Maryland state officials and policymakers regarding legislative reform and has provided written testimony to the United States Senate. Annie passionately advocates for child safety, collaborating with organizations like the National Safe Parents Organization and Custody Peace. She is the Board President of Family Court Awareness Month and is an active lobbyist for bringing Kayden's law into individual states. She was part of the team behind the passing of Maryland Senate Bill SB17 into law in 2022, which requires any judge presiding over a family court case involving domestic violence and/or child abuse to undergo 20 hours of specific training covering topics like trauma, child sexual abuse, and coercive control.

Connect with Annie Kenny:
Website: www.bloomconsultingsolutions.com
Facebook: https://www.facebook.com/BloomwithAnnieK
Instagram: @BloomwithAnnieK
Email annie@bloomconsultingsolutions.com

CHAPTER 8

IT HAPPENED, WE BELIEVE YOU

FIGHTING TO TELL MY STORY

Mary Jo Ross

MY STORY

I grew up in a generational satanic cult and was sex trafficked by family members in exchange for personal favors, grocery money, drugs, and cash. My dad played the director of "Teach Your Five Kids All the Ways to Have Sex." Thankfully, there are no videos or pictures.

The story of my "17 Years in Hell" could fill a book. The abuse started at my birth and ended at the beginning of my senior year of high school after I got kicked out over curfew issues.

I'll never forget being five years old and chanting, "I'm special!" as I danced and ran around. "I got a new dress! I get to go stay with my grandparents!" Granddaddy was taking me somewhere special to meet his friends.

That sunny, hot Saturday, I rode with him on the slippery front seat of his great big Cadillac to a place with a big parking lot. As we approached the building, I noticed there were no windows and a ruler and compass on the outside. Granddaddy held my hand and reminded me to make him proud.

Before I could ask anything, we were inside the building where nobody had their "inside" voices on. I entertained myself with a notepad, a pen, and a pencil during the meeting.

It felt like hours had passed when everyone got up and started moving around. While everyone took their chairs to the big room, I ran up to Granddaddy, "Is it time to go now?"

He said, "No!" He took my hand and dragged me through the big circle of chairs filled with all the men. He took me to the Grand Poohbah and, in a mean voice, said, "You will do what you are told. Make me proud."

Those men passed me around. I couldn't deal with it, so I went to a special place in my mind. I remember coming to and crying partway through the circle, "Please, can we go now?"

No one answered. I just got passed to the next man. My new dress was ruined. I hurt everywhere.

I learned later that Granddaddy got to move up in the organization's hierarchy.

About 40% of children who are sex trafficked are trafficked by family or someone close to them, including kids in your community. Head-in-sand reactions are common. If you acknowledge something is going on, you are responsible for doing something about it.

In my family, my grandfather, dad, mother, and older sister pimped me out. With five growing kids in the house, there was never enough food. My dad's construction company usually lost money.

Because males were more important than females in our house, they got larger portions and seconds. I was always hungry. Some Saturday mornings, my mother took me into town and dropped me off at one of two different places, depending on which man's turn it was.

Tick, tock, tick, tock. The grandfather clock at one house seemed very slow before I visited a field of flowers in my head for the next hour before she came back, and we went to the grocery store to spend the new cash in her purse.

After earning scholarships and going away to college to escape the family abuse, I went on to experience more abuse. I escaped with a broken relationship "picker." I chose relationships replicating my childhood trauma.

At 23, as a new mom in a miserable marriage and severely depressed, I started having dreams my dad was getting into bed with me instead of my husband. Curled up in a ball, pictures and feelings flooded in. I could barely function.

I couldn't spend one more night crying and calling hospitals when my husband didn't come home.

I can't live like this anymore. I need help. I don't want to remember or tell anyone, but I don't have a choice. I can't let my son be exposed to my family or what happened to me.

My husband's health insurance policy would cover mental health help, but I had to get a referral.

After several nights of not wanting to fall asleep and dream, I got the nerve to call my doctor's office to schedule an appointment. "I need to get a referral for a therapist," I told the receptionist.

"Who is your doctor?" she asked. "Okay. Um, uh, just a minute."

His nurse came on the phone. "Who is this? What do you want?"

"I need to get a referral. I need help because I was sexually abused."

"Really? Are you sure?" she said.

She thinks I'm dirty. I'm not a bad person. Why in the hell would I make something like that up?

The referral appointment finally got scheduled for three weeks later. Normally I could get an appointment within a day or two of calling.

My doctor knocked on the door before entering his office, where I sat. He put a file down on the table near the door, turned away, and walked with his back to me toward the window.

"What are you here for?" he asked.

"I need a referral. I was sexually abused, and I need help."

"Tell me what happened," he said.

"I can't remember."

"You can't?" He asked, "I need to know what happened."

Why does he need to know the details? He's not a fucking therapist.

"I can't remember. But I know it happened."

"Well, if you can't tell me what happened," he said, "you're just making things up for attention. You don't need a referral."

"I'm not making it up. I need help!"

He finally turned and looked at me. I didn't get out of my chair.

Then he said, "I don't believe you."

He finally agreed to refer me to a female psychiatrist he knew.

Two weeks later, I sat in front of her desk. "Why are you here?" she asked.

"I was sexually abused and need help."

"Tell me what happened," she said.

"I can't remember. I just know it did."

When she said, "If you can't tell me, it didn't happen." I saw red.

Not again! Why the hell would I make something like that up? I know it happened. I just can't remember. She sounds just like my doctor. I hate him.

Less than ten minutes after I arrived, the psychiatrist ushered me out of her office, "You're wasting my time." I started bawling as I left the office. I pulled over several times during the 23-mile drive home because I was crying so hard.

I decided to face the embarrassment of going to the community mental health center in our small town, where everyone could see who was coming and going. My puffy eyes, red face, and tears got a quick response. A therapist took me into a small room.

"Why are you upset?" she asked.

After I calmed down, she looked at me, "The doctors said it didn't happen. The only option I have is a 12-week group for Adult Children of Alcoholics (ACOA)."

I started the ACOA group the following week. Meanwhile, things got even more miserable at home. My husband was upset at having to "babysit" his child every week while I went to my appointment. He got angry when I started going to Al-Anon. "Don't you dare say anything about me. You're the one who's crazy and needs help."

He got fired from a large aerospace company when he forgot his ID badge and went to get a temporary badge while reeking of pot smoke. It was the last straw. I filed for divorce just a few days after finding out I was pregnant again.

My son and I moved out, couch-surfed, and were homeless for six weeks.

We ended up in an apartment which cost $47 per month. I qualified for Medicaid and food stamps since I was pregnant and in no condition to hold a job.

When the 12-week group was almost over, my ACOA social worker, Allen, introduced me to my hero and therapist, Carol. Carol had lots of experience dealing with child sexual abuse, as well as generational satanic ritual abuse. She became my lifesaver.

It wasn't an easy job for her. I wasn't an easy client. For me, it was exhausting and debilitating to uncover the memories which came flooding back. Once I began to peel back the scabs covering my childhood memories, the worst part was dealing with the satanic ritual abuse.

The generational satanic cult I grew up in but never knew the name of came through both parents. My mother was a high priestess, so her side was more powerful. Severe consequences hung over our heads to deter any talking.

As a result of cult programming that began at age two for my siblings and me, I still automatically turn the wrong way. It was deliberate to destroy credibility in case we tried to show someone where a ritual occurred.

However, Carol believed in me. Two of my sisters happened to be in therapy in different states at the same time and we all signed releases so our therapists could talk to each other. The therapists believed us because we told the same stories, just differing by roles and ages.

Most satanic ritual abuse survivors never have validation.

I'm not crazy after all!

My mother, the martyr, laid guilt trips to try to get me to visit her and other family members in another state. In a forwarded letter, she wrote, "I'll be happy to buy you a computer so you can work and keep in touch better. You need to get it in person. It's too expensive to ship."

I was glad we'd moved into an apartment. Our neighbor reported someone who looked like one of my brothers sitting in a car outside our former house for most of the week. I think he planned to kidnap us.

For our safety, and with the support of my therapist, social worker, law enforcement friends, and attorney, I severed all ties to my biological family. Not having a family left a gaping hole in my life for years. As a result, I stayed in relationships way past the expiration date, no matter how dysfunctional.

Since I divorced the ex-husband my mother feared, my son and I were extremely vulnerable because when you're born into a generational satanic cult, you're not allowed to leave and live. You have an "accident" or commit suicide, with or without help.

An AA member hosted a daily radio show on our local station. I agreed to be interviewed a couple of times on air so that it would be investigated if something happened to me. I couldn't disappear if my son was going to survive and be safe.

After those interviews aired, a friend introduced me to a lieutenant from the sheriff's office. We sat in her living room for two hours before the lieutenant looked me in the eye and said, "I believe you." I cried because it was the first time I'd heard those words.

The lieutenant introduced me to a homicide detective from a nearby police department who also believed me. It felt like I had bodyguards when I was their surprise guest speaker at a statewide law enforcement conference on generational and other satanic cults.

When my youngest was almost six months old, I learned I'd be losing my Medicaid benefits. Since Medicaid only paid for two hours per month, and Carol donated two hours per month, I drove 45 minutes each way twice a week for my 30-minute appointments. I took several medications that couldn't just be stopped suddenly.

I wasn't ready to get a job and support the three of us.

Damn it! There's got to be a way. I'm not giving up.

I researched our state government and got contact information for the governor and all the legislators involved in anything to do with health and mental health. I wrote the governor a letter cc'ing 17 people, asking, "How can you help?"

Two weeks later, my social worker called, "I've been told to drop my other cases until I can get you on Social Security Disability Insurance (SSDI)." Temporary help let me see Carol and take my meds for a couple of months until I was approved.

After three years of therapy, I "graduated" and re-entered the workforce. I worked with developmentally delayed adults in a community setting. Later, I drove an hour and ten minutes each way to work at a partial hospital day school which was a partnership between the mental health center and special education services.

As a case manager, I worked with severely emotionally disturbed adolescent males in a classroom with eight students and four staff. I also led a psychosocial group twice a day. My job included taking my clients out in the community and into their homes, as well as to any court hearings or IEP meetings.

I earned Employee of the Month several times and then Employee of the Year. My boss told me, "I've never known such a strong advocate for children."

In a desperate move, I got back together with my children's father, and we moved to Oklahoma for his job while I volunteered at the boys' school. The relationship finally ended when he raped me with his fist on the morning of a sunny school day. Our door was partially open, and the boys were awake in the other room. His reaction to impotence was violence. I ended up miscarrying not long afterward.

I found a new therapist. Two pastors and their wives helped us move into an apartment.

I worked two jobs to put food on the table because I didn't receive child support.

Eventually, I climbed the professional ladder and became executive director of six nonprofit state professional associations at the same time and owner of an association management company. Instead of doing drugs, drinking, starving, binging, cutting, or other things to avoid memories, workaholism was my coping mechanism.

It took extreme burnout and lots of effort to improve my coping skills and have a healthier attitude toward work. Now my business-consulting clients benefit from my hard-won wisdom.

THE PRACTICE

I've found when I share my story, it gives permission for others to share theirs. I'm always amazed at how many people have been sexually abused and have never told anyone.

Please reach out and tell someone what happened to you. Sharing your story will help you heal. You can write it out if it's too hard to speak the words.

If someone doesn't react sensitively to you disclosing, it just means they're not the right person for the moment. It still happened. **You lived through it.** No one else has the right to tell you your reality. It's important to find a compelling reason to tell someone else. I was determined to ensure my children were never exposed to anything I experienced.

Fight for yourself. Fight for your kids. Fight to break the cycle.

I didn't have any friends, so Al-Anon was the first place I found people who'd listen to me without being paid. There are lots of free or low-cost support groups. Many times, people in recovery were abused, often sexually.

It takes a great deal of courage for a survivor to tell their story, so I created a helpful handout for those who find themselves interacting with survivors. It's called **Tips for Dealing with A Survivor of Child Sexual Abuse, Familial Child Sex Trafficking, or Satanic Ritual Abuse.** A link to the worksheet is in the resource section. Here are some of the tips:

- Because every person is different and so is their experience, there are no black-and-white answers to help you support someone in their journey to survive and then thrive. It's important to sit back, breathe, and listen.

- Tell them, "I believe you," and "You are brave to share what happened to you."

- Tell them you're sorry the abuse happened and want to understand and help them.

- Remind them it was not their fault.

- Ask permission before touching them.

- If possible, stay at their level when speaking with or listening to them, even if you must sit on the floor or stand up.
- Any sexually based actions or innuendos are inappropriate.
- Realize that you'll probably hear only a small part of the abuse until they trust you.
- It's okay to empathize or sympathize, but DO NOT SAY, "I know how you feel," even if you think you do. It's a major insult.
- You may have experienced trauma and/or abuse. Please realize your experience doesn't match anyone else's. People handle trauma differently.
- It's better to stay away if you're going to be judgmental. You're NOT better than they are. You're fortunate not to have their experiences.
- If you're triggered by something you're told, it's okay to leave the room, but tell the survivor why ("I am sick to my stomach," etc.) so they don't take it personally.
- Keep calm. You may be very sad or very angry. Some tears are okay. It can be a trigger if you let yourself get caught up in anger and show it.
- If you're very emotional, remember that you're there for them. DO NOT expect them to help you deal with your emotions.
- If you don't have a local resource or don't know how to find one, The Demand Project is based in Tulsa, Oklahoma but has connections to resources all over the United States. Please go to their website, https://www.thedemandproject.org, or call them at 539.525.0191.

After surviving 17 years of severe childhood abuse, **Mary Jo** worked hard for many years to break the cycle and protect her children and others. Even though it makes people uncomfortable, she provides information about child sexual abuse and dares to bring up the topic in conversation. She strongly believes people who ignore it help perpetuate the abuse of children in our families and society.

A business owner since 2007, Mary Jo now helps other small business owners to do such things as preparing their businesses so the owner can take a "real" vacation.

Mary Jo enjoys travel and has been to 30 countries, all 50 states, and many national parks. An avid reader, she has read thousands of books and is finally writing books of her own. She enjoys being a member of the Burlington Better Speakers Toastmasters group.

In addition, Mary Jo volunteers with The Demand Project in Tulsa, Oklahoma, USA, which exists to eradicate human trafficking, online enticement, child sexual abuse material, and the commercial exploitation of children, through prevention, protection, recovery, and restoration. A 501©3 nonprofit, TDP provides services and resources for adult and child survivors across the United States.

Connect with Mary Jo Ross:

LinkedIn: https://www.linkedin.com/in/maryjorichardsross/

Website: https://www.maryjoross.com

Website: https://mjexecconsulting.com

Email: maryjo@maryjoross.com

Tip sheet: https://www.maryjoross.com/resources

The Demand Project

https://www.thedemandproject.org

contact@thedemandproject.org

call: 539.525.0191

CHAPTER 9

KILLING THE MONSTER

SILENCING THE VOICE OF SHAME AND GUILT

Val Meola, Author, CSA Advocate

THE MONSTER'S GAME

She's five years old, but she's not afraid of the boogie man,
Cause the boogie man knows her name.
They said to watch for strangers,
But a stranger never caused her pain.
She'd tell the ogre to go away,
But she's too little to complain.

So while she doesn't understand,
She plays the monster's game.
And now this beast lives in her head,
And is driving her insane.
She can't escape the boogie man,
Cause she knows the boogie man's name.

MY STORY

I was alone, sleeping quietly in my bed, when daddy playfully awakened me. His large hands tickled my belly and slowly moved toward my thighs and into my panties.

I asked timidly, "What are you doing?"

He replied, "It will make you sexy."

I was four, "What's that?"

He motioned his hands in the shape of an hourglass. I still had no further understanding, but I supposed sexy must be a good thing. Nonetheless, I had some clear sense that this secret was not right and that I could never tell anyone.

Having a mother who could explode at any time reinforced my need to keep my silence. Having been blamed and beaten more than once for things that weren't my fault or out of my control, I'd never tell. Besides, what would I say about something I had no concept of and no vocabulary to explain?

One time, after playing the monster's game, he gave me a $20 bill. I took it but had to pretend I found it on the street so I wouldn't have to explain how a ten-year-old came across so much money. The message now was clear. *This twenty was much more. It turned the child into a whore.*

For the next 12 years, waking up at night with my panties already removed and the sexual acts already in progress became a regular occurrence. I can't even say that during the early years, I feared it. It's just something that was. The grooming and the fear of my mother worked to the monster's advantage. Most of the individual encounters I can't recall specifically because, at some point, I learned to freeze in space and let my mind and body become separate entities.

I dare not say that, eventually, I'd become sexually aroused. Saying this for the first time evokes panic. My heart beats rapidly, my breaths deepen, and I shake slightly as I let tears trickle down these aging cheeks. I can feel this small child all over again. My little girl is saying, *Stop here. Let's run away.*

My lack of understanding of why these feelings occur was so rooted in my shame and self-blaming. *Will others judge this child? Did she want it? Was this consensual? I'm an evil child. If I judged and sentenced myself, certainly everyone else would have even stronger opinions.* I feel this small child all over again.

As the years went by, I became more and more uncomfortable with the abuse and was conscious that it was undeniably wrong. I wondered as I grew into my teens, *is this something that happens with all girls and their fathers?* It was the 1960s and 70s. I never heard anyone talk of such things. *How would we know what's normal?* Deep down, I knew it wasn't, and my awareness sent me hiding more inside myself.

I was stalked at every corner, on alert everywhere. One day, when done bathing in an old clawfoot tub with no shower, I looked towards the locked bathroom door where I thought I was safe. The monster's eye was peeking through the crack where someone had broken a panel. *I can't even take a bath. How long has he been doing this? He knows I saw him and doesn't care.* After that, I covered the crack with a towel before removing my clothes. Just months ago, I found out he had made another hole from the adjoining bedroom. I'm devastated that I didn't see that, and I don't know how long he peered through that hole. *His sickness never ends.*

As other men familiar with my family did similar things, my negative thoughts turned inward. *Did I have a sign on my forehead? Was I looking for it? Did I do something to deserve it? Why can't I just say "no?"*

Uncle Joe was in his late teens and nine years older than me when he started playing the same monster games in the basement of my grandparents' home. My older cousin, Wayne, fondled me when on an overnight visit.

Then there was Georgie, the nice old man in my parents' bowling league who handed out quarters to the kids. *Not so nice at all.* Just another monster who was taking children on the back steps and molesting them between bowling. He was caught. What happened to him? He was severely punished by having to leave the bowling team and told to get help. None of the children were helped as it was swept away. I never admitted to being one of his victims. *I'll probably be blamed.*

One day, not too long after this, my mother said to me, "I'm surprised it wasn't you with him." Those words haunt me. *What did she know? Was she blaming me for what she knew? Why didn't she protect me? And why did I protect her to her death?*

If my mother didn't know, she certainly should have. I believe, or want to believe, she lived in denial. Was he so good at covering up and explaining away the most obvious signs and events that she couldn't see what was right in front of her?

There was this dreadful night in my early teens. I was in that frozen state with my mind far away. The monster, with his fly open, lay across me on my bed, his feet still on the floor. I was ripped back into reality when she grabbed him by the neck. "What the hell are you doing to her?" Then they both disappeared into the night. I lay there the rest of the night, wanting to die. Was I in trouble? Will I be beaten? Will I be questioned? Will I be blamed? When is she coming back in here? Maybe I could run away. The wait was worse than any outcome that might have happened. She never came back, never mentioned it, ever.

> The monster's execution had been stayed.
> There was relief in being so betrayed.
> The reality is I would have lied through my mask.
> But at least I would have known she cared enough to ask.

I was 16 when one night, I did something that would change things. I had been trying to fight him off for a few years. On this particular night, my mother was staying over at a friend's house. I told him "No," but he wouldn't give up. I didn't freeze like before. Instead, I ran to the door and down the marble steps to the sidewalk. He must have stopped to put shoes on because there was a short break before he came out after me. I could see him gaining on me as I ran down the city streets turning the corners, hoping to lose him. He was getting closer. I turned a corner. *I'm trapped.* I crouched down between two parked cars waiting to be caught. To my surprise, he walked right past me. I saw him, but he didn't see me. His sights were set down the long city block.

Now what? Where can I go? Nowhere. I'd have too much explaining to do. That can't happen. What now? I returned home sometime later. The monster was asleep. He never came at me again. *Hmm. He's afraid of being exposed.*

Life moved on, and I played out the charade of the normal, successful, and dutiful daughter. I moved out at 18 and worked my way through college. I went home for every holiday. I bought my parents gifts that were usually more than I could afford. At Sunday mass, I'd kiss him on the cheek at the sign of peace as though I could forgive him. I did everything against my instincts that said *to run away,* all to keep up the image I wanted everyone to see.

I married at 23; I let the monster give me away at my wedding. I danced to "Daddy's Little Girl." I did all the posed daddy/daughter photos. 8x10's in the wedding album. *That's normal, right?* Bile rises in me. *Why did I do this to myself? At least no one would know my secret. I'm the good girl.* A great disguise for the guilty, dirty feelings hidden inside the sardonic mask.

> *If I am innocent of the crimes that I was made from*
> *Then why, in the end, does absolution never come?*

Shortly into my marriage, I did share with my husband, Michael, what my father did. He was very supportive. He had great instincts to protect me, but I made him promise to keep my secret. *I don't want anyone to know what I did. I need to continue donning my mask.* There was not much mention of it over the many years except when I'd be awakened by my own screams from nightmares reliving the monster's games.

Ten years ago, I got a birthday card from my parents. It should have been something beautiful. It said I was a daughter they loved and cherished. Something about my generosity and what a great daughter I am. *Blah, blah, blah. File 13 for this load of crap. Vomit or cry? Both.*

Thirty years of marriage, two great kids, loving friends, a successful career, and a nice home could never quite fulfill me. I just knew I didn't deserve all those blessings because of what I had done. *One day, it will all come out, and you'll lose everything and everyone. You're a phony.*

Feelings were pushed down into a dark hole. I told myself this was never going to affect me. The little girl was never allowed to cry. This supposedly mature woman would not be angry or sad. *No feeling sorry for yourself.* I thought I was protecting her, but I was wrong in so many ways.

THE PRACTICE

Almost 50 years after the monster stole my childhood, I finally found this voice that the child never knew she lost. I slowly began uncovering the skeletons in my closet that were locked away so tight. I took tiny steps leading me out of the monster's shadow that obscured the truth.

It began one night after having a conversation with my best friend, Kathy.

Me: "I was molested when I was little." *Why don't we call this what it is? Rape.*

Kathy, in a shocked voice, "Oh my God! Who?"

Oh, crap. I should keep my big mouth shut.

Filled with shame, "Um, I can't say." *I might lose my bestie. What would she think? Incest is so hideous. She'll think I'm repulsive.*

Kathy: "Someone I know?"

Sobbing, "Yeah."

Kathy: "Don't tell me because I won't keep your secret." *Ah, she would want to stand up for me.* I managed a little smile to acknowledge my understanding.

Driving home that night, I composed the poem, *The Monster's Game.* I went straight to my office to write it down before I forgot it.

I don't know what I expected to find when afterward I opened my browser and very slowly tapped my overgrown nails on the keys: "I N C E S T" search. It was as though I was being driven to DailyStrength.org/incestsurvivor within a few clicks. This may have saved my life. I hid suicide ideations for 30-plus years.

For the next year, I holed up in my office alone each night, reading, writing, and crying. Initially more reading than writing, but the anonymity was the safety I needed to open up in this new place where everyone gets me. *How could these sister warriors, Ausie, Carolin, Amy, Lakin, and others, know me better than my family and friends? Better than me? They do!* They taught me so much, typing about words that previously had little meaning to me. "You weren't willing; you were groomed." "You disassociated to protect yourself." "I see the inner child." "Trigger warning." They were real in this virtual world. "I hear your screams." "I see your tears." "I feel your pain." "I've got you wrapped in my arms." The once scary place was now my retreat.

Night after night, I was Lisa, who could only speak in rhyme, from the play *David and Lisa,* I saw as a teen. All my memories recorded in cadence and rhyme. Writing my worst memories in poetry, I could mask the harshness. *Still playing it safe.*

I examined my story over and over again as I turned these poems into a book. It was a painful process, but I don't regret it. *There was some pleasure in feeling so sad.* But something else surprised me. I was angry. *That damn monster hurt that little girl. And her mother did not protect her. She was just a baby. She was helpless, defenseless, scared, and voiceless.* I reached that child and, for the first time, saw the world through that little girl's bright blue eyes. She became a victim instead of a whore. *Hey, shameful little voice, you no longer get to occupy my thoughts. I'll no longer ignore you. I'm ready to take you on. Send that shame back to the monsters who own it.*

Healing did not come in a day, a week, or a year. Melting away the shame was like burning the wax from a jar candle. You light it and swish around the liquified wax. But not too much, or the flame will be snuffed out. The heat transforms fluid into gas, causing it to evaporate. Maybe some soot settles nearby. When the candle is extinguished, the wax hardens once again, but each time it's relit, more of the wax dissipates until the jar is empty and can be discarded forever. The wax is my shame hardened in my head. The flame liquefying the wax is my voice. The candle would burn for varying lengths of time and remain dark in between as I needed to step away. Before I even realized it, the shame vaporized, leaving little residue to be washed away.

The work on my healing journey was not yet over, though. I freely shared in the safety of online groups, but I didn't know how to share with those closest to me. *If I open the dam, the water will drown everyone in its path, and I'll not be able to close the locks. I don't want to be responsible for that. I can't ruin the lives of those I love. How can I even approach it? Just blurt it out one day? Besides, how could I answer questions they were too afraid to ask?* That's the story I had created in my head, but in reality, the fear of telling was worse than the actual disclosure. The fear of losing people I love never happened. The disclosures hammered away those guilty messages in my head.

I stumbled into making something good from evil along the path to healing. Although I caution that just because you can sugarcoat them by making lemonade, it doesn't make the lemons any less tart. I turned my attention to advocacy by participating with NAASCA, RAACE, and Shattered Canvas. I was called to speak on local TV, blog talk radio, and to a church group in Washington, DC. My career took me across the US, Aruba, Brazil, and the UK, where I was fortunate to meet with many sister survivors. These beautiful women remain close in my heart no matter how infrequently we talk. I'm frequently reminded of this quote from survivor Faith Reagan: "Alone, we're a whisper. Together, we're a roar."

The real shame of my story is that it's not unique. It's sadly a story I share with millions of adults and children worldwide. I chose to focus my advocacy work at the RAACE Foundation, located in my hometown in Maryland. In 2019, I became president of the organization and have a mission to reduce the number of victims through knowledge. We're developing tools to educate parents, teachers, clergy, and anyone that cares for and about children. The facts of CSA can dispel myths, and caregivers can be better informed about how to prevent the monsters from entering their circle of trust. With a focus on communication between parents and children, we know that an informed child is a safe child. These tools are also a message to perpetrators. *We're watching you.* Admittedly, we have much work to do, but our dedicated organization is determined to make a difference. *If I can save one child from enduring this life of torture, it will be worthwhile.*

My work in prevention and survivor support gives me the strength to continue facing my monsters. I have to believe in myself as much as I believe in what I do.

If you would like to know more about preventing CSA, reach out to RAACE.org for a free *Power of Prevention Guidebook.* Join our team by becoming a RAACE Hero.

For my survivor sisters and brothers, light your candle. Give yourself the time and space you need to empty that jar of shame. I hope you can kill the monster living in your closet and live the life you were meant to have instead of the one dealt to you.

Val is the author of *The Monster's Game*, written under the pseudonym littlegirl413. She is also a contributor to the anthologies, *Letter to a Monster* by Caroline de Chavigny and *Purple Sparks* by Stephanie Y. Evans and Sharnell D. Myles. She was featured in multiple issues of *Memoirabilia* magazine in 2014.

As a CSA advocate, she is the current President of Race Against Abuse of Children Everywhere (RAACE). As a speaker, she hopes that her voice resonates with other survivors, teaches all who care for children, and warn the monsters that they can no longer hide.

Facebook page: The Monster's Game

Email: littlegirl413@yahoo.com

RAACE Website: RAACE.org

CHAPTER 10

RESILIENT

THE TENACITY OF A LITTLE GIRL
AND BECOMING AN ADULT THRIVER

Kim Lakin Creger

MY STORY

It started as a beautiful fall day in Colorado. My friend and I finished riding our bikes and went inside. We decided to go to her house, where she lived with her uncle and aunt. The basement was a fun place to play. At some point, while we were playing, her cousins came home. Suddenly, I was confused. The younger cousin, who I knew "liked me," had given me love notes and record singles and now had me in the closet. I remember wondering what was happening. Then, his pants were down, and I could see everything. OMG! What should I do? I was only five years old. It's when the first abuse occurred.

• • •

My mom was sixteen, and my dad was eighteen when I was born. While my mom finished high school, we lived with my great-grandma Chrisman in South Dakota. By the time my mom was twenty, she had two children, my brother and I; had moved to Colorado, and got a divorce. I did not see my biological dad, Keith, again for many years. And I never called him dad. My brother and I spent many summers with my grandparents (Keith's, my bio dad's, parents) in Arkansas, and we might see Keith if he happened to be in town. He never made any effort.

I was three when my mom met my stepdad. I remember feeling like my life had changed. I was now in charge of my little brother and had a lot more responsibilities.

We lived across the street from a family with a little girl the same age as me. We would play at each other's houses, with most of our time at her house as I lived in a little one-bedroom. My friend had a whole basement where we could run around and play. I remember the two male cousins of my friend would walk around their house with their pants unzipped. I thought it seemed odd, but my parents were open, so I guess it seemed normal.

While visiting my friend one day, the brothers separated us. One of them, the one I knew liked me, wanted me to touch his penis. I ran out of the room as fast as I could. On my way upstairs, I saw my friend being abused by her other cousin. However, in my five-year-old mind, I thought, *she must be more mature than me.* From then on, I avoided going to her house.

When I was about six, my grandmother found a church that would pick up my aunt and me (we are two years apart) and take us to Sunday School. I loved getting all dressed up for Sunday School. I always felt very safe and happy when I was at church. It was a nice break from home. I believe this foundation is what helped me to be able to start to heal.

Shortly after starting Sunday School, I got extremely sick. It took about a month to figure out what was wrong. My doctor kept saying everything was fine and that I must have something going on that I was hiding or something was happening at school, so that is why I didn't want to go to school. Both of those things were correct. However, something bad was also happening in my body that almost killed me. I was in so much pain. When they finally figured it out, my appendix ruptured. I was an extremely sick little girl for about nine months—in and out of the hospital and having two operations. I missed most of the second grade. This would lead to me being held back in third grade, another traumatic life event for any child.

After recovery, we moved a few blocks away from my friend. My friend came to my house to play.

Between the ages of eight and twelve, a cousin would visit from out of state. While we played an innocent game of hide and seek in the dark, he would touch me. Not knowing at that time that it wasn't right, I thought, *all guys must do this stuff. Isn't that what girls are for anyway?*

At twelve, my stepdad sexually abused me. It happened at the same time he was getting ready to adopt us. Later, he told me that he stopped because I told the judge I wanted my stepdad to be my dad. I did not know I had any choice in the adoption. I went to Arkansas a few months earlier with relinquishment papers to give to Keith, my biological dad. And felt so guilty that he was upset. He signed them. He passed away about a year later. I lost any chance of ever getting to know him.

By thirteen, I was interested in boys and ready to be free from the sexual, mental, and physical abuse in my home. There was always marijuana in our house, shared with the children, weird religions my parents tried, and parties that involved a lot of drugs. I have thought of my childhood as living in a hippie, free-love type of atmosphere. Great for pedophiles and druggies but not so much for children.

At fourteen, we moved to Washington State to open a restaurant with our family. I met my first real boyfriend at the restaurant and fell madly in love. All I wanted was to escape. While sneaking out to meet him one night, my parents caught me. My dad threw me through the wall, and I decided it was time I told my mom what he had done. I don't remember everything; however, I remember her saying, "It happens." She told me that she had been abused as a child as well. I remember thinking, *what does that have to do with me?*

I became rebellious after that. My boyfriend and I ran away to Florida for three months. I eventually left him and came back to Littleton. I then found myself drugged and raped at another friend's house one night. I felt so betrayed.

At nineteen years old, I became a single mom. I knew I wasn't going to let my daughter fall into the same abuse and lifestyle I had growing up I also met my husband while I was pregnant. That's another story. The unconditional love my children and grandchildren have given me is the biggest blessing I could ever have.

I've spent years in various kinds of therapy and counseling. It is a continuous healing process.

I've always felt that I would be an advocate for child sex abuse prevention. It has also been healing to talk openly about my abuse and teach adults to be proactive and how to protect children from child sexual abuse.

THE PRACTICE

Did you know that one-in-ten children will be sexually abused before their eighteenth birthday? An abuser could be the person sitting next to you at work or someone volunteering in a youth group. We need to be the voice for those who need help articulating their truth. Believing the child is the first step to any healing. Understanding that sometimes traumatized children will act out or have episodes of acting out will help caregivers understand where they're coming from. Acting out is usually a sign of wanting attention.

My heart is to help educate adults about CSA prevention by providing training to our community, the Colorado region, and our online community worldwide with our nonprofit Darkness to Light, Stewards of Children.

We can start empowering our children to have future generations without child sexual abuse.

I have had the honor of training over 700 adults, parents, staff, and volunteers at churches, schools, health centers, youth-serving organizations, and more in D2L, Stewards of Children.

We can all make a difference by helping adults take proactive steps to protect children from this risk.

Adults are responsible for the safety of children, so adults are the ones who need to prevent, recognize, and react responsibly to child sexual abuse.

Yet the statistics clearly show adults are not shouldering the responsibility.

Why are we at such a loss when it comes to protecting children from sexual abuse?

Most adults don't know how to recognize the signs, and many do not know what to do when sexual abuse is discovered.

Darkness to Light (D2L), Stewards of Children is a two-hour class for adults, designed to help you to understand all these questions and more.

Stewards of Children is an evidence-informed, prevention, solution class that increases knowledge, improves attitudes, and changes child protective behaviors. It offers practical prevention training with a conversational, real-world approach.

Stewards of Children® has been extensively evaluated and is the only evidence-informed child sexual abuse training program available nationally.

Why is this program different?

Stewards of Children uses real people and real stories to show you how to better protect children and watch out for the signs of abuse.

• • •

IMPORTANT CONSIDERATIONS

Making Choices

We all have the ability, both in our organizations and in our families, to make proactive choices that protect children and keep them safe from sexual abuse.

Taking Risks

Sometimes we must take risks to protect children even if we are uncertain or don't know the outcome.

Supporting Each Other

As communities, organizations, and individuals, we can support each other's efforts to prevent child sexual abuse, and we can ask for support when needed.

These are what make up the Five Steps to Protecting Children.

Even if you were not sexually abused as a child...
...even if no one in your family was sexually abused...
...child sexual abuse impacts everyone's life.

The average lifetime cost per victim of sexual abuse is over $210,012.

These expenses are largely paid for by the public sector – the taxpayers.

The US spends $124 billion annually on the costs of sexual abuse.

These costs include:

- health care costs
- criminal justice costs
- child welfare costs
- special education costs
- productivity losses

Add this to the fact that sexual abuse is the root cause of many other devastating and expensive social problems, such as male survivors of child sexual abuse being 70 percent more likely to seek psychological treatment for issues such as substance abuse, suicidal thoughts, and attempted suicide.

Except for murder, child sexual abuse is the most expensive victim of crime in America. And we all pay. Prevention is the answer.

At least 60 percent of victims are abused by people the family knows and trusts.

About 75 percent of child pornography victims are living at home when photographed.

Physical signs of sexual abuse are not common. Emotional or behavioral signals are more common. These can run from "too perfect" behavior to withdrawal and depression, to unexplained anger and rebellion.

You most likely know a child that has been or is being abused.

DISCOVERY of sexual abuse means you've witnessed a sexually abusive act by an adult or youth with a child, or you know by some other means that abuse has taken place. Report your discovery immediately!

SUSPICION of sexual abuse means you've seen signs in a child or witnessed boundary violations by adults or other youth toward a child.

OFFENDERS are rarely caught in the act of abusing a child, but they're often seen breaking the rules and pressing boundaries.

Sexually abused children who keep it a secret—or tell and aren't believed—are at greater risk than the general population for psychological, emotional, social, and physical problems, often lasting into adulthood. You likely know an abuser. The greatest risk to children doesn't come from strangers but from friends and family.

MINIMIZE OPPORTUNITY

Understand that abusers often become friendly with potential victims and their families, enjoy family activities, earn trust, and gain time alone with children. This is called grooming!

Think carefully about the safety of any isolated, one-on-one settings. Choose group situations when possible.

Think carefully about the safety of situations where older youth have access to younger children. Make sure that multiple adults are present who can supervise.

Set an example by avoiding isolated, one-on-one situations with children other than your own.

Monitor children's Internet use. Offenders use the Internet to lure children into physical contact.

Insist on screenings that include criminal background checks, personal interviews, and professional recommendations **for all adults who serve children.** Avoid programs that do not use ALL these methods.

Insist that youth-serving organizations train their staff and volunteers to prevent, recognize, and react responsibly to child sexual abuse.

Ensure that youth-serving organizations have policies for dealing with suspicious situations and reports of abuse.

ONE-ON-ONE TIME with trusted adults is healthy and valuable for a child. It builds self-esteem and deepens relationships.

To protect children while nurturing these relationships:

- Drop in unexpectedly when the child is alone with an adult or another youth, even if it is a trusted family member.

- Make sure outings are observable - if not by you, then by others.

- Ask adults about the specifics of planned activities before the child leaves your care. Notice their ability to be specific.

- Talk with the child following the activity. Notice the child's mood and whether he or she can tell you with confidence how the time was spent.

- Find a way to tell adults who care for children that you and the child are educated about child sexual abuse prevention and body safety. Be that direct.

- Parents need to have age-appropriate, open conversations about our bodies, sex, and boundaries.

- Talking about personal safety and sex creates a protective bond between the parent and child, increases confidence for both, and instills knowledge that makes the children and teens much less vulnerable.

- Understand why children are afraid to tell. Often the abuser shames the child, points out that the child let it happen, or tells the child that his or her parents will be angry.

- Sometimes children who do not initially tell are ashamed to tell when it happens again. Children are afraid of disappointing their parents and disrupting the family.

- Some children are too young to even understand, or they love the abuser and don't want to get anyone in trouble. They just want the abuse to stop.

KNOW HOW CHILDREN COMMUNICATE

- Children who disclose sexual abuse often tell a trusted adult other than a parent. For this reason, training for people who work with children is especially important.

- Children may tell portions of what happened or pretend it happened to someone else to gauge adult reactions.

- Children will often "shut down" and refuse to tell more if you respond emotionally or negatively.

Talk openly with your child.

- Age-appropriate, open conversations about our bodies, sex, and boundaries give children a foundation for understanding and developing healthy relationships. It also teaches them that they have the right to say "no."

TALK WITH OTHER ADULTS ABOUT SEXUAL ABUSE

- Raise the consciousness of your community and influence their choices about child safety.
- Offer support and information to an adult whose child is experiencing abuse and may not know what to do.
- Put potential abusers on notice that you are paying attention!

REACT RESPONSIBLY

- Disclosure, discovery, and suspicions of sexual abuse provide opportunities to intervene on behalf of a child. It's also the moment when children learn whether others can be trusted to stand up for them.
- Do not overreact.
- If a child breaks an arm or runs a high fever, you know how to stay calm and where to seek help because you've mentally prepared yourself. Reacting to child sexual abuse is the same.
- Children may feel ashamed, guilty, or shut down. If they don't feel heard or believed, they may change their story, when in fact, the abuse is occurring.
- Offer support
- Think through your response before you react. You'll be able to respond in a more supportive manner.
- Believe the child and make sure the child knows it.
- Thank the child for telling you, and praise the child's courage.
- Encourage the child to talk, but don't ask leading questions about details. Asking about details can alter the child's memory of events. Seek the help of a professional who is trained to interview the child about sexual abuse.
- Assure the child that it is your responsibility, as the adult, to protect them and that you will do all you can to help them!
- Report or act in all cases of suspected abuse, both in and outside of the family.

- Making Choices, Taking Risks, Supporting Each Other - all these build the 5 Steps To Protecting Our Children. We can make a difference!

- Get trained - Darkness to Light (d2l.org) for more information or to sign up for a class. Classes are available online.

- MBF Child Safety Matters - Monique Burr Foundation Monique Burr Foundation (mbfpreventioneducation.org) The National Association of Adult Survivors of Child Abuse at www.naasca.org

Kim is a mom to three grown children and six beautiful grandchildren.

She is honored to be a Darkness to Light, Stewards Of Children, Certified Instructor, and Authorized Facilitator for the past seven years.

Kim enjoys speaking and has a heart for mom's groups and churches.

Kim became an author a few years ago with her testimony in *The Stories Of Roaring Faith, vol. #5.*

Kim is a NAASCA Ambassador and Stop Child Abuse Now (SCAN), Blog Talk Radio Show Host at www.NAASCA.org.

Kim is also an authorized facilitator for The Monique Burr Foundation for Children. Teaching body safety.

And the CEO at Kim Lakin Creger and Soar on Eagles Wings.

Contact her at email: info@kimlakincreger.com

Website: www.kimlakincreger.com

Follow on Facebook at Kim Lakin | Facebook and

Soar On Eagles Wings | Facebook

LinkedIn (16) Kim (Lakin) Creger | LinkedIn

Kimberly Lakin Creger (@kimlakincreger) • Instagram photos and videos

CHAPTER 11

BECOMING VISIBLE
COMING OUT OF THE FOG

Strong Oak Lefebvre, Ko'asek Traditional Band of Abenaki, NH

MY STORY

Knowing where the shotguns are and believing in our visions are critical to our safety and healing process. We know a lot about lies. We know about not telling people that we are a "two-spirit" so we don't lose our life, home, or job. A "Two-Spirit" in indigenous communities is a person who is both male and female. We know about being forced to wear clothes that hurt our spirit. We use the pronoun "we" to honor our nonbinary identity.

A long time ago, when we were two years old, our mother tied us to a tree in our front yard. Then, she abandoned us there and went into the house. We worked the knot until we made our escape. Such joy and liberation! Walking down the sidewalk, we were stunned to see a giant metal round cover tossed aside, exposing a hole in the sidewalk. To the left of the metal cover, a head, detached from a body, stared at us with a smile. We looked behind us, scared and knowing this scene was just not right. The sidewalk looked normal. We looked in front. The head and metal cover were still there. We knew the scene was not real. A voice spoke to us. "Do not tell anyone about this." This scene is one of the many visions we'd have.

Another time, we felt engulfed in bliss, twirling around in a much-hated dress our mother made us wear. We thought: *Nothing in our life can explain this feeling.*

We lived in a prisoner-of-war home where no one could breathe or speak. Our father was a rageful alcoholic who molested us, hit us, and verbally abused us. We lived in dread.

Another time, we cried because our brother threw a stone and hit us in the corner of our right eye. Our father flew into a rage, grabbed us by the front of our dress, and lifted us off the ground, ripping our dress. We were paralyzed. There was fear in his eyes. He dropped us to the floor and rushed out of the house. We see him pacing in our grandfather's yard next door. He looks distraught. At that moment, we both knew he could kill us, thinking: *Why does he hate us so much?* From that moment on, we knew becoming invisible was vital to survival. We let no one in.

Invisibility is essential when in a situation with no means of escape. Children have no power. *Who would believe us? Things will get worse if we call the police or tell anyone.* We could be separated from our families, or worse, we could die. We know shotguns are in the house and where the bullets are. We decide to use the gun if our father crosses a line. We will go to jail to make it safe for everyone else.

We know about not being visible in history books and the big lie of Columbus. The thread of invisibility runs deep. The lies are structured into a racist construct that forces indigenous people to have a specific blood quota to determine our existence. The memories of the residential boarding schools reside in my DNA. The truth is in my DNA, and the healing lives there too. We know our father was a sexual assault survivor and was in a Canadian boarding school when he was a child.

Our intergenerational memories forge a bridge between the present and the past by accessing the wisdom of our ancestral knowledge. Ceremony can take you there. Our very first ceremony is in a sweat lodge. The journey begins there. The sweat lodge is a recreation of the world. Saplings crisscross to form a circular structure containing four spiritual knowledge levels. It looks like a wigwam, only much lower to the ground. We cannot stand in it. Inside, there is a carefully tended hole about three feet in diameter. The firekeeper brings in the hot rocks. They've been meditating in the fire for several hours in the fire pit outside the lodge. They carry messages and memories. The firekeeper stays with the fire and the rocks. When they're entirely red, the firekeeper brings them into the lodge. In indigenous culture, men keep the fire, and women hold the water. In the lodge, the water poured over hot rocks produces steam.

Our ancestors are present to hear our prayers and guide our healing process. We are very hot, with steam coursing down our breasts. After the second round, the medicine woman asks, "Does anyone need to come out?" We don't know how to answer. We say, "We feel extremely hot." The intercessor says, "That is what you're supposed to feel. You're okay." So, we stay. In the next round, we feel cold! It's then we know the Creator is a natural and accessible presence. Those in attendance are invited to ceremonies in South Dakota.

A month later, we're in South Dakota on the Pine Ridge Reservation, attending ten days of purification ceremonies with the Chips family near Eagle Nest Butte and five miles outside Wanblee. We're greeted by Phillip Chips and told where to pitch our tent. We choose a place in the West direction. Then we take in the ceremonial grounds. Men are repairing the roof of a building that has uneven walls. A water pump sticks out of the land, with a puppy tethered. A long, thick orange electrical cord extends over the Earth from the ceremony house to a refrigerator housed under an outdoor cook shack covered with tree boughs. We learn that a big storm knocked down the mobile home that was supposed to serve as the center. We encounter a woman with nasty bruises over her arms and face. We ask, "How did you get those?" "Phillip did this, she replies. We're waiting for our family to pick us up." We stand together in silence in a pact of understanding. As we meet others, we learn how members of the medicine family are impacted by drugs, alcohol, and domestic and sexual violence. *Oh my God, we're trapped in our family of origin with no means of escape. We have no access to a phone and no ride to the airport.* It's just me and the spirit that lives in all things now.

That evening we drift into dreams. Invisible souls travel wooded trails, their energy fields beautiful in their seamless connection to Mother Earth. Their moccasins make no sound and leave no trail. The edge of confusion disrupts the beauty of their energy wheels. There is a spirit dilemma of feeling forsaken, a medicine not working. They're pursued by pale ones who are aggressive, greedy, and grasping. These pale ones move through the woods on paths they did not make. It's the clash of cultures that defines this confusion.

In the dream, our family drinks beer around a fire, drowning their pain, seeking to forget who they are and what they've lost. The women and children are bruised, bearing the misdirected anger of their loved ones.

We awaken in the pre-dawn hours, dripping with sweat and fear. We see the forsaken dog tethered to the water pump, barely able to stand in the emerging light of the sun. We watch the sun slowly elevate as though it's rising from the Earth's bowels on the distant horizon. We feel like that dog, alone, miserable, untouched by humanity.

People have come from around the world to participate in healing through the Yuwipi ceremony. We make prayer ties for those who seek healing. Sweat lodges for men and women are done before entering the ceremony house. Men sit to the left of the entrance. Women sit to the right. Those seeking healing sit directly across. The medicine man, the Wicasa Wakan, lays on a bed of sage, hands tied behind his back, covered with a buffalo robe. Food is in the center and is part of the altar with sacred objects for healing. The Yuwipi ceremony is done by those who inherit the medicine as a birthright. The drums and prayers begin. Rattles fly through the air by themselves, untouched by human hands. They touch those receiving healing—all pray. There is drumming and chanting from the medicine family members. Then the Wicasa Wakan's hands are unbound by the spirit, and he throws the buffalo robe toward attendees. Then the food is shared by all, and the ceremony ends. We then learn that the *dog tethered to the pump was sacred food for the ceremony.*

We were puzzled. "How can those who cause harm also be the ones who heal others? How can the Creator allow that?" Those questions were born of anger, rage even, at the idea that our father could be a healer. It led us to a transformative journey to discover how that could be.

It takes over three decades of taking risks to explore ceremony as a path to recovery from trauma embedded in our DNA memory as an indigenous person. We're called to Wisconsin to attend the "Women and Water Coming Together Symposium" at the Lac Courte Oreilles. We know we're in the right place when the host tells us, "Put away your notebooks. This is sacred ceremonial space; what counts is that you listen fully and integrate your experience." They offer us a chance to heal through the Wiping of the Tears or the Jingle Dress ceremonies. We stand in a line before a medicine man who makes that decision after hearing why we're asking. We don't even remember what we said, but we were assigned to the Wiping the Tears Ceremony.

We gather in the healing lodge the following day and place our gifts on a blanket. Eleven of us are individually brought with loving care to our chairs, three to a row. Three healers are seated in chairs before us. The healing drum begins, and the medicine man prays and sings. We begin to vibrate, front to back. Next, our hands start to vibrate. Our body is shaking and quaking. Tears are flowing with no reference to a particular memory. We think: *This has been going on for a long time. Will my body stop vibrating?* We are not scared. The hands vibrating was exhilarating.

One by one, we were brought to one of the healers. When seated there, a support person surrounds us with a blanket that assures our privacy. Our shirt is removed. A healer washes our face and hands. We feel the love of our ancestors for us. To say we feel nurtured is not enough. It's like being welcomed home, free of seven generations of grief. Then our socks are removed, our feet are washed clean, and new socks are given to us. Being cleansed from the blessed water in copper cups washes me clean of grievous memory from seven generations of ancestral harm. We're not the same. We're gently guided back to our seat in the second row of three chairs. After everyone has completed the ceremony, all dance around the lodge, greeted by our community of supporters. We forgave the Creator; we forgave ourselves for the harm we have done; we forgave all those who ever harmed us. We now understand how we, too, can be a healing force in the world even though we are not perfect.

THE PRACTICE

An essential part of our healing and recovery involves decolonizing ourselves and learning about the world before the settlers came here, massacred us, and raped our children in the residential boarding schools. Those traumas live in our DNA; their healing needs more than sitting in the office of a mainstream therapist or counselor. It needs indigenous healing practices.

We founded our agency, the Visioning BEAR (Balance, Equality, and Respect) Circle Intertribal Coalition, Inc (VBCIC). By 2015, we had our own 501 (c) (3) organization to prevent sexual assault. Indigenous survivors formed the board. Together we co-authored a prevention curriculum called Walking in Balance with All Our Relations: An indigenous primary prevention approach to healing both those who harm and those who are harmed based on indigenous values and traditions. https://visioningbear.org

Transforming the culture of power is critically essential for our healing. It gives meaning to our life to support the journey of others. We teach about the Doctrine of Discovery and the Papal Bulls of 1493 that gave Columbus a command to take away lands from any people who were not Christian and to place them into perpetual slavery. The structure the colonizers created in separating from England stated that only white property owners could own property. Women and people of color were not allowed to vote or get an education. Ultimately, capitalism became the currency of poverty, where all beings, plants, animals, and humans, were objectified. The colonizers own the plants and animals without their consent.

Through VBCIC, we host *Transformative Healing Circles* that address healing those who are harmed and those who commit harm. Those who abuse need healing from the pain that leads to violence. They need healing, not retribution and incarceration. The Great Law of Peace of the Haudenosaunee Nation teaches us that until those who harm are healed, violence will not end.

We build drums. When we drum, we calm ourselves from emotional upsets. We also use drumming to travel to spiritual power animals and to journey to teachers in the Spirit World. We work with our hands, bead, paint feathers, and brain-tan animal hides to make our regalia. The brain of an animal is just enough to tan its hide. In these ways, we claim our power.

We spend many hours connecting to the land. We walk the land, seeing signs that speak to us of our spiritual connection. Indigenous people believe that plants and animals are our teachers. They agreed to help human beings before the first woman came here. Our first task was to learn about the four medicines: Tobacco, sage, cedar, and sweetgrass.

Participating in sacred, traditional ceremonies keep us in tune with living according to the Seven Grandfather Teachings. Those teachings are love, respect, courage, humility, compassion, wisdom, honesty, and truth. Honesty and truth are not the same. Truth is a lifelong pursuit that cannot be achieved without honesty. Learning to speak honestly, especially in the face of conflict, is vital for our healing. Dealing with conflict requires love and compassion to effect lasting change.

We want to cross the river to the Spirit World without the emotional baggage of the trauma we experienced. We want to forgive God, forgive ourselves, forgive everyone we harmed, and forgive everyone who harmed us. Then we will be free.

Strong Oak Lefebvre is the Executive Director and co-founder of the Visioning BEAR Circle Intertribal Coalition INC. She is a co-author of the *Walking in Balance with All Our Relations* teaching curriculum, a violence prevention bystander approach based on indigenous people's traditional values before colonization. The curriculum is designed to decolonize indigenous peoples and reclaim historical ways of being in the community. The curriculum speaks of historical trauma and is meant to serve as a way of being in indigenous communities that would prevent the incidence of all forms of violence. It is also designed to be embraced by multicultural groups seeking an intersectional understanding of structural racism and how it informs the prevention of sexual and domestic violence.

Strong Oak, LICSW, has a master's in social service administration from Case Western Reserve University School of Applied Social Sciences. Lefebvre served on the Advisory Council for the National Sexual Resource Center from June 2010 to June 2016. While on the Advisory Council, Ms. Lefebvre was its voting representative to the Pennsylvania Coalition Against Rape Board of Directors from 2010 to 2013. From 2016 to 2020, Strong Oak represented VBCIC, one of ten organizations nationwide, with the Just Beginnings Collaborative. This funding organization seeks to build a nationwide movement to end childhood sexual assault. Transforming communities to embrace restorative practices in dealing with both those who are victimized and those who have victimized others are essential aspects of Strong Oak's work. She teaches Circle process to communities, agencies, coalitions, and providers working with survivors of homicide victims, domestic and sexual violence, and those who harm them.

Strong Oak can be contacted at https://www.facebook.com/strong.oak.7
https://www.linkedin.com/in/strong-oak-lefebvre-806b86b7

CHAPTER 12

RELEARNING THE STAIRS

A FINE LINE BETWEEN LOVE AND HATE

Beth Donahue

MY STORY

We had to have one ear and eye open to the stairs. We knew the abuse would start as soon as the last creak of the stair hit. We listened and waited.

We were in our rooms having contests. We whispered to one another: "Am I in handstand position?" We timed who stayed up against the wall the longest. Then came burping contests. I learned to say my grandmother's name in a burp. I won the contest every time. We were grounded for days and had to come up with contests to make the time go by. All the while watching the door and listening to the creaks on the stairs.

We had each stair down pat. The creaking got louder as my father climbed them. He tried to be quiet, so he caught us by surprise. We learned early to listen to every noise and became attuned to listening, smelling, touching, and seeing. Our senses are still as strong today.

Once he had his way with us, we'd either be allowed out or grounded again for another week. This continued through our adolescent years. I was grounded from report card to report card. Abuse affects all aspects of a child's life, including school. My grades were horrible, and my father used this as a tool, with my mother's permission, to ground us. My mother never questioned why our grades were bad. She called us "bad kids."

As the only daughter, I was put in the mother role while my mom pursued her career and was gone as much as possible. My father had all the power; he manipulated us and kept control—for about ten years.

We ran away a lot and were brought back home. We had school activities. As we got older, my father manipulated our involvement to control and abuse us even more.

I went to church with my grandmother at an early age. I always felt a presence envelop me when I got there. I loved that feeling because it made me feel safe. I clung to it when I left the church and learned over the years to use what I called the 'sleep blanket' to fall asleep. I relaxed in bed. I stared at my feet, put an invisible blanket around them, and wrapped it up my legs, around my torso, and over my chest. I started at each arm's fingertip, brought it up my arms, met it at my chest, and then continued it up my neck, face, and head. I was completely locked into an invisible blanket that gave me peace to fall asleep. I still use this sometimes today. It was interrupted when my father came into my room in the middle of the night to molest me. I tried to fight him, but the threats came. He would say, "It won't hurt; you know I love you, and I will let you go out tomorrow when you get home from school." While he molested me, my brain went elsewhere, and I thought about happy places, like being at the beach. I did this until the molestation finished, and he left my room—a form of disassociation from the abuse.

This is partly why I had trouble in school. He was abusive in all ways possible: Mental, physical, and sexual. It took years to figure out how to get past it all. I hated him while he was abusing me and knew I had to get away from him as soon as I was old enough. When I was ten, I ran away for the first time and prayed, "I hope I never have to go back there again." He beat me badly enough during "the last time" that one of my friend's sisters called the police, and they took me to the police station. I had welts and strap marks on my back. My mother came and told the police, "She's using drugs." They could tell I wasn't. I stayed at my grandmother's that night, then flew to my aunt's the next morning and lived with her for a year.

Most predators don't change their stripes. My father tried to get me home after the year, saying he'd "never touch me again." He lied. It wasn't long after I got back that he tried to molest me again.

I learned tools as I grew. I learned how to escape into my mind while the abuse was happening. When something terrible happened, I mentally tried to escape it by any means possible. Escaping became a coping mechanism. I got better and better at it as each incident occurred. When he came into my room, I knew I had to be mentally prepared. I played scenes over and over in my head to try and get it to stop. I'd say to myself: *He's not got power over me; he's going to get caught; maybe he'll die.* But nothing stopped him. I started to blank out and try to forget what had happened, but that was impossible. I was thankful when my period started. It meant that, for at least a week, I wouldn't be molested.

I started reading a lot to get into something else besides my own life. Reading about what life was like for other people helped with my daily trauma. I could either relate or wish I was with the characters in the book to keep me safe. It was another coping skill to escape the pain. I carried reading skills with me for life. I still read to this day, but not the type of books I did as a kid. I read healthy books that can change my life by helping me make lifestyle changes. I also like suspense novels. Reading stories that had no bearing or impact on my thought process put me in a mindset of forgetting life for a while. When reading, the world disappears. I can read a paperback book in a couple of days. When I'm done, I feel relieved I could leave the world for a while; I feel rejuvenated. One of my teachers, Ms. Prizio, I'm indebted to. She taught me to speed read and gave me extra time in school to sit in her classroom and read. She understood.

I began running away regularly. This became a consistent pattern throughout my whole life. Any time I was abused, I got to the point where I couldn't take it anymore and didn't care where I had to live. Sometimes, I got picked up by the police, and they brought me back home. I planned my next escape as soon as the abuse started again. It was a lifecycle I carried into adulthood. That's where my being a nomad came from; I must have moved 30 times in my adulthood.

Young kids should never have to learn survival skills like a military service person. My father was never in the military but used different military tactics on us. He hid a toothpick on a piece of furniture to see if we found it or had us look for Comet on the sink, toilet, or tub to indicate we didn't clean fully. That was his excuse to ground us again.

I learned anger and defiance at an early age. I learned how to stand there and not cry. I learned to do what I was supposed to do based on his sensibilities, to which he demanded I comply. I learned how to love and hate, which can form a very fine line. I thought about ways to kill him. I thought about things I could do to stop the abuse, but I had no control over that. He always found ways to abuse me. Until I got to an age where I didn't have to go home again, I had to do what he wanted and act as if nothing was happening.

I finally ran away permanently. I lived with a friend and her family and finished high school. I'm forever grateful to them for saving my life. I lived with my aunt and uncle for a year. I lived with a girl from school for the last two years of high school. I learned at a young age what being a nomad meant, and I knew my clothing had to work in any season because I'd be in the cold for a while. All I wanted was for the abuse to stop.

Once I moved out permanently. I thought, *everything is going to change now.* The abuse stopped, and I had great people to rely on and help me. I had friends who knew about the abuse and who I could talk to about it. Talking is so important when it comes to trauma. Most people hold it in, which is very dangerous. It eats at your soul and can destroy you from the inside out. At some points during those years of abuse, I used drugs and alcohol to escape what was happening. I'm very lucky and thankful that they didn't carry into my adulthood as addictions, and I can function without their use as a crutch.

But there are various types of addictions. Drinking, drug addiction, and other vices like food can become critical showstoppers in healing. They're crutches that help people get through each day. I was one of those people. I worked and ate carbohydrates to feel better. I went out on weekends with friends, drank, and danced in clubs. *This is how I'm supposed to be,* I thought—*having fun, loving life, and being with my people.* This lasted through my 20s, and I knew it had to change as I got older. My father was an alcoholic, and I knew I didn't want that for myself. I forgot everything when I drank and danced. I put on weight and before I knew it, I gained 78 pounds and was now 214 pounds. I didn't like the way I looked or felt, and something had to change.

I decided to go to counseling. It didn't click with the first woman. I wasn't comfortable talking to her. I didn't feel comfortable or safe opening up about things.

I decided to try another counselor, and we hit it off immediately. I could talk about the things that happened. She gave me assignments. I went to her for about a year and gained a foundation. Boundaries were the first block I was missing: I didn't have any, and that's why my relationships were always in turmoil. Once I learned to keep people out of my space and speak up for myself, I started healing. I ran with this for a few years. I looked for a sexual abuse survivors' group in my area, but there wasn't one. I decided to start my own. I was really nervous but knew it would help me and others.

I held the first meeting and announced it as "for survivors only." The meeting started well. There were five of us there. I started with the 12 steps. Then we went around the room, and each person identified why they were there. One guy announced he was a survivor and an abuser. It got really awkward, and the meeting ended. No one showed up the next week or the week after, and I ended the group.

I was angry because he'd shown up even though I underlined that the group was for *survivors only.* I took it as a learning lesson and was proud of myself for trying to get a group together. It was another first step for me, and I accepted it for the challenge it was. It gave me the strength to know I'd succeed in healing and helping others heal.

As the nomad I am, I moved again and decided to go back to counseling. This counselor was even better than my last. She was older and had great insight. I was like a sponge listening to her. We were there one day on a holiday. No one else was in the building. I started getting into some deep subjects about my dad, and, all of a sudden, the lamp with a pull-down on-and-off switch went flying. It was a chain with a ball on the end of it. Both of us looked at each other and laughed nervously. I realized that maybe his spirit was still alive and haunting me. That feeling lived with me for a long time. Years later, I brought sage, lavender, and myrrh to his gravesite and burned them while I told his spirit to get back in the grave. To this day, I'm not sure it worked. But I don't feel a presence around me anymore.

I've learned I'm an empath and believe it's because my mind had to go to other realms while being abused. I'm in tune with others, and people seek me out. As I get older, I'm more open to talking about the abuse I suffered. When someone tells me they've been abused, I make sure to listen to them.

I can tell where they are in their healing process. I give them information on what steps they need to take. I tell them my story, the different things I've tried over the years, and the strength I took from each life event.

THE PRACTICE

Take back the power. I did, and I have helped many more do the same.

In 2013, a group of us got together and decided we would embrace our strength and create an organization called The Innocence Revolution. It would be a global group that disseminated information from all groups across the globe, and we'd also hold a worldwide event during April (Child Abuse Prevention and Awareness Month). We developed a website with a calendar, and all organizations could list their events on it; anyone could use and keep track of what pertinent events were going on. It was a great success in 2014. We had 26 countries hold events, and we even had one event posted from churches in Italy (Vatican-approved) about a rummage sale. I felt we were on the way to success with ending child abuse as we knew it. We got the most powerful organization in the world on board! Since then, we had some targeting issues arise due to the sensitivity of the topic, and some people resigned. That's about to change. We will be back and operational by the time this book is published.

I've been trying to create November 3rd as "All Survivors Day" so we can have locations across the globe for people to meet up and talk to one another when we need to. The reason I picked this day is because it coincides with All Souls Day and All Saint Day. I think it's important to have a day for everyone who has survived abuse, be able to hear others, and tell our stories. Legislation will be created and submitted to create this day.

I want to finish by saying every victim can become a survivor. There are many practices you can try. Below are some of what's worked for me and others.

First, you need to know yourself.

- Learn boundaries first. That means when to be touched and when not to. Know the space that is comfortable (and uncomfortable) for you to have someone stand in and put that space in between you and another person.

- This includes verbiage. Don't let someone treat you in a way that makes you feel uncomfortable. You have to speak of it with the other person. Verbalize nicely. Do it a few times with yourself, and be strong and comfortable with your words.

- If you feel like there's too much stress, meditate. Take back your senses. Let the stress leave your body by finding a space only you can sit in. Light candles and stay in your safe space. Try this once a day.

- Go to counseling if your world is spinning out of control. Make sure you feel comfortable with the counselor. It may be awkward at first because no one wants to open up about abuse, but you have to. If, in three or four sessions, you still cannot talk, find another counselor. Perhaps you'll need a counselor of the same gender.

- Exercise. You will have a lot of anger during the counseling. The best way to vent it is to walk, use a stepper, jog, etc. Find your exercise and use it to your advantage to get out the pent-up anger.

- Give yourself credit as you accomplish each task.

- Mindfulness - Don't blame yourself. Look into CBT (Cognitive Behavioral Therapy). It works.

- Write a letter to the perpetrator and put the responsibility back on the perpetrator. If they're not alive, write it anyway. Transference of the mindset of abuse from you to the paper addressed to the perpetrator is huge.

- Analyze your food, drug, and alcohol intake. Is it healthy? If not, what is making you eat, take drugs, or drink? Write it out and balance it one line item at a time.

- Try not to be afraid of the abuse that happened to you. It happened. My motto is, "You own IT. It doesn't own you or mold you. YOU mold yourself."

In closing, there are three little girls and two little boys, in particular, that I love to pieces. I hope someday you read this and know it wasn't your fault and that you are wonderful children. To the kids in my family, who I love dearly, I tried to protect you because you needed protection from your uncle. I want you and other children to be strong and know that there are people to protect you. I got involved with the laws to keep you safe, and so your lives would be normal without abuse. I know you don't understand that as a child, but someday you will. I work hard to abolish the statute of limitations, so none of you will ever suffer what we had to. I walked away from the family to do this. I love all of you. I relearned how to navigate the stairs. Please join me in helping others do the same.

Beth Donahue was born in Hull, Massachusetts, a beautiful seaside town south of Boston. It's bitterly cold in the winter and swimmingly friendly in the summer. She was lucky because she had the beach and a wonderful amusement park to play and work in each year. She made some lifelong friends who are still with her today. If it wasn't for them, she'd probably, like other survivors, not be here.

Beth finished high school after five years while living with other families to help her get through the disaster of her life. She worked a few jobs to make ends meet and learned the ropes of life. She still struggles some days.

Beth earned her degree in Computer Science and worked in many sectors of business doing technical support work through the years. She loves technology and watches for different technology-driven mental health techniques to learn about.

Beth always knew her goal in life was to help others. She helped start a global organization that helps stomp out childhood sexual abuse and works with legislators to change laws for the protection of children. She's currently proposing two pieces of legislation that'll help victims and survivors everywhere. She wrote a book about the abuse we all endure.

Beth also works with other groups to bring disaster relief to hurricane-hit areas. She finally bought a home and is out of the Nomad status. She wants you to know that you can change from a victim to a survivor, also. Thrive to feel alive.

You can connect with Beth at:

LinkedIn URL - www.linkedin.com/in/beth-donahue-6b87691aa

Email – bethdon01@hotmail.com

Facebook – The Innocence Revolution | Facebook

LinkedIn – The Innocence Revolution | LinkedIn

URL http://www.theinnocencerevolution.net

CHAPTER 13

FREE TO SPEAK YOUR MIND

FACE YOUR WORST MOMENTS WITH CONFIDENCE IN FIVE MINUTES

Christy Heiskala, CA

MY STORY

The teenage girl stood up and dropped the bomb that would forever shatter the world as I knew it. *Who is that? I'd never seen her before. She's much older than our girls.* Mr. Firth never made eye contact as he sat handcuffed in his orange jumpsuit behind the glass wall. She shared how he had molested her, too, years before her sister. As she returned to her seat, the judge read Mr. Firth his sentence, "You are hereby sentenced to…" Racing thoughts and questions flooded my brain while the judge's words faded.

With the slam of the gavel, the packed room erupted. Cameras were clicking as the crowd began to empty. I pushed passed the reporters shoving a microphone in my face and chased the girl down the narrow hall. "Excuse me, I'm sorry to bother you, but I have to know, what year did you have Mr. Firth?" When she answered, I quickly did the math and realized she had him in his first year of teaching. My daughter had him in his seventh year of teaching. It felt like a punch in the gut; the wind was knocked right out of me.

Seven years?!

How many more kids did he molest?

How did the school not know?

They had to have known!

They either knew and did nothing, or they weren't paying attention.

They could have stopped him before he got to my kid!

I'm getting a lawyer!

I spoke to the other victim's parents, and they agreed we needed to hold the school accountable for being so negligent. We met with an attorney. He explained the only way to prove the school was negligent was to get access to Mr. Firth's employment records. That required a subpoena which can only be obtained by filing a civil lawsuit against the school district. The attorney asked, "Do you have the strength to fight this?" I didn't even have to contemplate it; there was no question in my mind. This mama bear was ready to fight fearlessly for her baby girl.

A year passed before we received proof of what my gut told me that day in the courthouse. Mr. Firth's employment file revealed several parents reported his inappropriate behavior with his students over seven years. One mother told the principal her daughter complained the teacher had pulled on her underwear. Another mother demanded the school stop the teacher from playing his musical chairs game, where the winner got to sit on his lap for the rest of the day. The assistant principal wrote a disciplinary action after she found Mr. Firth in his classroom with the blinds closed and the door shut, alone with a third grader on his lap.

Two years passed before going to court. Mr. Firth struck a plea deal with the prosecutor, so he was released from prison by the time we went to trial. The criminal justice system let us down every step of the way from the moment my daughter reported, so this trial was our last hope for justice. The stakes were high because the school district made us an offer to settle the day before the trial. The offer was three times the amount of money my attorney told me initially that my daughter could get. That was before my daughter and I spent two years being deposed, psychologically evaluated, and painstakingly waiting for justice.

I refused to settle because we'd have been silenced by a non-disclosure agreement. I wanted the truth to be told, and I wanted the public to know, even if that meant she didn't get a dime. She didn't even know a civil trial was about punishing the teacher and the school district by making them pay money. I was seeking justice, not money, for my daughter from day one, and nothing was going to stop me.

Four weeks into the trial, I started having panic attacks. I regretted my decision not to settle. Even though it was never about the money, I suddenly feared all my daughter and I had been through might be for nothing.

Why didn't I just take the offer?! That was so dumb. How can I forgive myself if we lose and my daughter gets nothing after we were offered more than I ever expected? How will I pay for her to go to college? I am a terrible mom.

My entire body was riddled with pain from sitting there, day after day, in those hard wooden chairs, white-knuckling the armrest. Sending daggers in my mind to the defense attorney while he droned on for hours, telling the jury that my daughter was "damaged" long before her teacher molested her because she came from a "broken home." Being divorced was hard enough. I felt enough shame of my own. I didn't need this man telling the world I was a bad mom and my daughter's pain was all my fault. *Screw you! You don't know the sacrifices I've made. How dare you blame this on me. I am a good mom! How is this even legal?*

I studied the jurors' faces looking for any clues as to what they were thinking. My ears rang so loud I was sure the mom next to me could hear them. I clenched my jaw so tightly that I ground my teeth down, causing permanent damage.

Regardless of the hundreds of hours of testimony by dozens of experts and witnesses, the burden of proof weighed heavily on my shoulders because we filed our lawsuit past the statute of limitations. We missed the deadline to file a lawsuit against the school. The teacher molested kids for seven years, but the law only gave us one year to hold him and the school accountable.

Unless we could prove the school district kept us from seeking a lawyer.

It didn't matter that Mr. Firth pleaded guilty and was convicted. It didn't even matter that there was tons of evidence and witness testimony proving the principal and assistant principal knew about Mr. Firth's sexual misconduct for years. If we couldn't prove the school district prevented us from talking to an attorney, we'd lose our case. The entire fate of our trial rested on whether the jury believed me.

Each day, I looked at every juror and sent them positive energy and thoughts of gratitude for their service. I visualized thanking them individually when the trial was over for believing my daughter and me.

Thank you for taking this time out of your busy life to bear witness to our pain and my daughter's experience that should have never happened. Thank you for holding the school district accountable and finding in favor of the plaintiffs. I will never forget you.

I wondered if the jurors knew we were required to sit quietly and not react to anything being said. If I was on the jury, I'd have questioned how a mother could sit there listening to the testimony from her daughter's kindergarten teacher and therapist without showing emotion. Certainly, they have watched courtroom dramas on TV where mothers are sobbing out loud and yelling in defiance during testimonies. If the lawyer was lying, surely the jury would expect me to cause a ruckus. Sometimes the tears flowed no matter how stoic I fought to remain. My only outlet was to scream at the top of my lungs during the hour drive home from court every night.

"Next week, it is your turn. You will be the last person called to the witness stand." The knot in my throat almost choked the life out of me. The courthouse was closed on Fridays, so I had the next day off. Feeling beaten down, I wanted to surround myself physically and mentally with strong female energy. I decided to attend a workshop at the female co-working space where I belonged. The topic that day was public speaking and how to stay grounded while delivering a strong message.

How perfect, the universe must have known I needed this right now.

As the speaker shared that her organization helps courageous women who had been victims of abuse turn their life around, tears streamed down my face. The weeks of trial came crashing down hard, and I sobbed during most of her workshop. Generously, she let me be and continued. With a wet face and runny nose, I listened and remained present. I knew I was exactly where I was supposed to be. I thought she'd be giving tips and tricks for speaking to an audience, like how to stand or what to do with your hands. I didn't realize the key was a grounding technique.

In the days following the workshop, I practiced what I learned. While I sat watching the attorneys question witnesses, anxiety riddled my body. My cuticles were a bloody mess. *Breathe! Relax your jaw!* I visualized the grounding technique in my mind over and over as the trial was coming to an end; soon, I would be on the witness stand.

I don't know if this grounding technique is working. I'm going to keep practicing and visualizing anyway. It's all I got.

I woke up that morning fretting over what to wear, knowing the jury would be judging everything about me. I practiced the grounding technique while watching myself in the mirror. *You got this. You are a warrior. You will be victorious!*

I stepped up to the wooden box. The room looked so much bigger. My heart was pounding in my chest so hard I thought I might have a heart attack right there. Part of me welcomed death so I could be free from the burden I carried. I looked out at the sea of faces, desperately wanting to speak to them. I had so much I wanted to say bottled up inside; if you shook me, I would have exploded. Instead, I planted my feet firmly on the wooden pedestal, took deep breaths, and visualized the grounding technique in my head. As I went through all the steps, I began to feel strong. My heartbeat slowed, my body calmed, and I was ready. *I can do it. I got this!*

The next week, the jury's verdict was in our favor. As my pent-up emotions began to bubble to the surface, my body released a swell of tears. Jurors asked if they could hug me as they walked out of the courtroom. I vowed to take that experience and make a difference in the world. I quit my job almost immediately and began teaching child sexual abuse prevention to schools and parents.

As I traveled the world speaking at conferences, I used the grounding technique I was taught to help me feel calm and steady, so I could speak to crowds without my voice cracking. Other speakers saw me practicing the technique and asked me to teach it to them. Other healers shared their processes with me.

I became a victim advocate helping child sexual abuse survivors and their families navigate the criminal and civil justice processes. I helped thousands of survivors face their challenges one at a time. I took what I learned along the way and created the grounding technique I'm going to share with you.

THE PRACTICE

"Get yourself grounded,
and you can navigate even the stormiest roads in peace."

~ Steve Goodier

In uncomfortable or anxiety-producing situations that require you to be present, grounding techniques can help calm your nervous system and make you feel more secure. Beyond grounding, this practice will help you go from feeling powerless to powerful.

Stand in a safe space. Spread your feet on the ground at a distance that feels comfortable for you.

Open your arms wide and put your hands up towards the sky in the shape of the letter V. Keep your arms in that position throughout the practice. You can choose to keep your eyes open or closed.

Imagine that roots are coming out of your feet, anchoring you to the Earth. Your roots grow deep below the surface and will help you weather any storm. They spread far and wide, keeping you aligned. Your roots have absorbed everything you need from the Earth to grow.

Feel your roots nourishing you, traveling up your legs. You feel stronger and stronger as the nourishment travels to your gut. Your core feels strong and stable, like the trunk of an oak tree.

As the nutrients travel up to your arms, green leaves begin to grow one by one. As the leaves begin to cover your branches, they show you how far you have come. Each leaf represents your ability for rebirth and new growth. Your ability to produce and flourish.

As your branches continue to reach up to the sky, the wind rustles through your leaves. The tips of your fingers begin to tingle.

You feel the warmth of the sun on your face. Your neck is loose as your head gently rolls with the wind, slowly rocking side to side.

Your arms are steady as they sway with the wind, bending ever so slightly but never breaking because they are flexible and hydrated.

The clouds are gone as the sun clears your mind. Your belly feels full as you breathe in oxygen. With each breath, your lungs expand, and your heart is illuminated. You are glowing.

The wind is still there, but now all you feel is the warmth of the sun. Your skin is soaking it all in, nourishing you. You begin to radiate that warmth.

Your leaves absorb the oxygen from the air while your roots absorb the oxygen from the Earth. Your breathing is now in rhythm with the Earth.

Your throat opens and expands with each breath. Your throat is clear. The exchange of oxygen and energy is flowing through your body, feeding you, nourishing you, strengthening your trunk, expanding your branches, lifting your arms to the sky, clearing your mind, and opening your eyes, bringing you clarity and calm. You feel peaceful and present. You feel strong and stable. You feel calm and steady. You are ready. You are here now.

Repeat this mantra as you hold your pose:

Strong and stable,

I am able.

Calm and steady,

I am ready.

With each breath,

I am here now.

Christy Heiskala is a survivor who taught her daughter to speak up if anyone ever touched her inappropriately. When a teacher sexually abused her daughter in the third grade, she did exactly what Christy taught her, and together they stopped a predator who had been molesting his students for seven years. Christy spent the next eight years navigating the criminal and civil justice systems fighting for justice for her daughter. That led to Christy leaving her career behind and becoming a credentialed advocate who helps survivors of sexual assault and child sexual abuse navigate their path forward. Christy also mentors survivors who have healed and want to become advocates.

Connect with Christy:

Go to https://www.advocateforvictims.com/how-to-become-an-advocate to find out about Christy's next book: *How to Become an Advocate, Turn Your Pain into Your Profession, and Get Paid.*

Go to https://www.advocateforvictims.com/contact to request a hand-painted watercolor graphic for use as a visual tool for the process.

Go to https://www.linkedin.com/in/christyheiskala/ to connect with Christy on LinkedIn.

CHAPTER 14

FROM VICTIM TO GODDESS

AN EMBODIED PRACTICE FOR ULTIMATE CATHARSIS

Christy Young

MY STORY

There were always a lot of people at the lake house where I spent my childhood summers: cousins and friends of varying ages came and went all the time, and the place operated much like a summer camp, filled, as it was, with ongoing activity. There was cooking in the kitchen and the fixing of boats and other repair work happening down by the lake. People fished, went boating and canoeing, and there were games of horseshoes and croquet that gave way on rainy days and evenings to board games and backgammon, cribbage, and gin rummy.

It should have been idyllic. Except, for me, it wasn't.

All that bustling activity provided the perfect cover for my paternal grandfather. He waited until he was alone with me in a semi-secluded setting and then seized the opportunity to molest me. The sexual abuse he perpetrated happened over many years and began when I was somewhere between five and nine. I could have been younger; I'm not sure. The truth of the matter is that the abuse robbed me of my innocence and many memories.

Alone   *Isolated*   *Paralyzed*

This is not unusual, and statistics further say that 49% of sexual abuse victims are under the age of six. The younger the child, the more likely their abuser is a family member. What's more, some child molesters have admitted they're less likely to abuse children who know the proper names of their private body parts and who've learned basic body safety skills.

Strangled   *Suppressed*   *Subdued*

My grandfather was inconspicuous, of course: predators are usually very good at lures and disguises. He operated covertly, as the coming and going of all our guests and visitors provided a large amount of distraction. Beach towels were large enough to cover any private areas and any foul play or inappropriate touching. As far as I know, nobody suspected a thing.

Trapped   *Muzzled*   *Stifled*

Predators choose their victims based on vulnerability, obedience, kindness, loyalty, and trust, and I was—check—all the above and a perfect unassuming target for my grandfather's hideous intentions. Publicly, he created a reputation above reproach, making his behavior even less likely to generate suspicion. He even won the "Man of the Year" award in his hometown!

What a fraud, a chief masquerader, I remember thinking later.

The award celebrating his integrity–in the form of a black and white plaque—hung in the kitchen of the lake house, making a cruel mockery of the experiences I endured at his hands. The fact that he was beloved, respected, and even revered by many people in his hometown gave him a certain amount of what's known as the "VIP factor" that so often accompanies predators. Many of the sexual predators who abuse young children are well-known local leaders in schools, athletic and civic organizations, and houses of worship. This makes it more difficult for victims to report them, as they feel the added pressure of bringing a public accusation against them.

Gagged   *Muted*   *Restrained*

In my case, if at any point I had publicly come out with an accusation against my grandfather, I believed there was a strong probability my parents, siblings, cousins, aunts, and uncles would not have believed me. So, I remained quiet. I carried a terrible secret around with me for decades.

In fact, nine out of ten children do not tell anyone they've been sexually abused. Because the abuser is often a family member, the child may be dependent on the abuser for basics like food and shelter, or they may fear breaking up the family. They may have been threatened not to tell, so they're afraid. Many survivors feel a sense of embarrassment, shame, or guilt over what happened. They may mistakenly believe they're somehow responsible, that they did something to make the abuse happen.

I did tell my mother about the abuse some years after my grandfather's death when I felt I needed to speak out to someone. It's by the grace of God that my grandfather's abuse did not affect me negatively when it came to my relationships and intimacy. A clairvoyant told me recently this was because of my connection with the divine and my ability to receive divine guidance, even at a young age. During a session with her, she said, "You seem to have been given an ability to come above it, to know what is in the highest to do; with your painting you just did it, with your husband you just did it. You have a clear connection to what you ought to do, to know what to do; it's a clear line to divinity. It's a very beautiful way of being."

Unafraid   Empowerment   Clarity

Those were comforting words, and I felt the truth of what that wise woman said. These dramatic experiences are given to us so we may have an opportunity to grow, gain wisdom, and become resilient. I absolutely do realize these intense experiences can also leave us feeling extremely fragile, almost like we might break in half. They can take us down to the depths or, conversely and miraculously, they may activate us to rise higher. I don't know if it was an actual conscious choice for me to thrive in the wake of my experiences or if perhaps I was blessed by the hand and grace of God. Much as I would have preferred my grandfather choose not to consume my innocence with his depravity, today, I've derived clarity from the confusion and pain and the courage and strength to forge on in the face of the horrible betrayals and vile acts I experienced. I tell my story to liberate the dark secret I held. I don't need to carry the shame of it all, either.

Luminous   Released   Free

I hold hope and have faith that other sexual abuse survivors and victims can move from the windowless, dark halls and walls that once closed them in, to find their way to a clearer, brighter space and place, and to embody a lighter way of being. There is a way to get there, and I'm living proof it can be done. One vulnerable step at a time. Our life is a tapestry woven from our personal experiences of sorrows, fears and tragedies, joys, and delights, too. We're here to experience it all—and it has *everything* to do with how we rise from the fall. It's how we keep going, how we keep moving through it despite the things that can so easily be our ruin, to not let it break our very spirit and soul. I am the sum of all my parts: my broken self, fused, soldered, and repaired. I'm all of it, the battle wounds and the scars. I've always loved this quote by Ralph Waldo Emerson: "We acquire the strength of that which we overcome." It rings so true to me. My hope for you is to know the strength it takes to walk through the mire, having survived those circumstances, that you remember the courageous and magnificent being you are, and that you are proud of where you are currently standing, here in your power.

THE PRACTICE

I was a very shy and introverted child, and I kept many things to myself. I've learned over time, however, to speak my truth as it helps me heal. Having gone through the heartless and inhumane experience of childhood sexual abuse (and subsequently thereafter having a string of romantic relationships with men who were physically and emotionally abusive), I ended the cycle. I set firm and healthy boundaries and, in the process, started on my healing journey.

Initially, I began studying the healing art of Reiki and joined a small painting school in New York City. The sense of belonging the arts and healing communities gave me also helped me expand on my strengths. I read some impactful personal growth books and went to talk therapist appointments weekly; I journaled and maintained a vigilant yoga practice. But perhaps the thing that had the most powerful effect on my healing journey was a practice I created all on my own, in quiet solitude.

Ceremony has been used for centuries by every culture to honor, respect, and mark a passage or rite. It can be used to honor beginnings and endings, to let go of the old and bring in the new, and can accelerate the pace of these changes. Ceremony can also be used to offer gratitude and appreciation to the Universe. When we are at a crossroads or in the middle of a transition, ceremony can help us to celebrate joy and release sorrow.

A ceremony does not have to be elaborate and complicated; in fact, sometimes, the simpler the message you send out, the better. You'll get the most benefit from ceremonies by incorporating them into your daily life. I call one practice I particularly like "Pitching it to the Universe."

You can start this ceremony by first heading out into nature. I usually go to a wooded park with a river nearby as there is something deeply cleansing about rushing water. Next, find a stone and hold it in your hands. Just sit still and meditate, and ask Source to be with you; quiet your thoughts and either close your eyes or hold them partially open, in a relaxed state. Draw upon what you want to bring into your life and equally pull up those things you wish to release now and forever. These are fervent prayers, and when I started using this practice, I found the process enormously cathartic in the darkest period of my healing.

Next, holding the stone, take a deep breath and blow into it deeply, starting from your lower abdomen and rolling all the way up through your lungs and out into the stone. Do this three or four times, turning the stone each time. Then, making sure you have a clear path, *pitch it!* Sit in stillness for another moment; you have officially turned your intentions over to the Universe.

Many years after the traumatic period of my life had ended, and having moved through a tremendous amount of difficulty, I now have a sense of wholeness and peaceful serenity. I have found myself. I value and love myself. There will still be times, of course, when I will be challenged. However, the toxicity in my life has vanished; it has been transmuted. I have joy and the freedom to work and explore my journey of personal growth. I also have the physical mobility to explore the beautiful world outside my door. I will never take these things for granted. The grass is green, and the sky is blue, and I have free will to choose, to creatively craft the life I want to live, to be bold and brave, and to summon the courage to love with an open heart.

I have a book in production with an editor and soon to be published called the *Handbook for Healing*. It is a ten-step guide that will assist you on your individual journey to find greater calm in your heart and more peace in your mind. Look for it in online bookstores in the spring of 2023!

I am an artist and a certified Reiki Master with numerous degrees, certifications, and training experiences that have led me to joyfully merge art and healing for the benefit of my friends, family, and clients.

In 2013, I opened Hummingbird Cottage Art Centre in the settlement of Hope Town on Elbow Cay, working as director of the Art Centre and Gallery. We held classes and workshops for adults and children, bringing in both foreign and local instructors, and we hosted lectures and gallery openings, as well as weddings and musical events. We were recommended in notable periodicals and travel guides, and we were honored when the National Art Gallery of the Bahamas asked us to showcase a retrospective show of the now-deceased, native Bahamian artist Amos Ferguson in the spring of 2017. Sadly, however, I had to sell the business soon thereafter during my divorce.

Since 2018, I have facilitated workshops in the Bahamas for hurricane survivors suffering from PTSD after Hurricane Dorian devastated so much of the islands of Abaco. I have also worked with chronic pain sufferers, pre- and post-op surgery patients, people in hospice and end-of-life care situations, epilepsy patients, women in labor, and clients seeking overall general body and mind alignment sessions. More recently, I have begun to offer weeklong wellness workshop retreats in the Bahamas and continue to offer private Reiki sessions and group classes in guided meditation and restorative yoga at my studio in Richmond, Virginia. I continue to paint in my studio in the Flatiron district of New York and in my home studio in Richmond, Virginia. I work mostly in oils and with a variety of subjects. I am working towards a solo show with an exhibition slated for early 2024.

And I am the proud mother of three creative children.

www.christyyoung.org

Instagram: @christyyoungenergywork

www.christyyoungartist.com

Instagram: @christyyoungartist

SHH, BE SILENT, CHILD

Shh, be silent, child
don't speak
of the pain you've suffered
and endured
the adults, they will not believe you
"a grand imagination!"
"such a storyteller!"
they will say.

Yet I want to speak of
perversion and molestation
but mostly confusion.
Grandfather
you weren't supposed to do that
and where does that leave me,
a sodomized child,
with a broken, irrevocable
family trust
rescinded,
redacted.
And I, the beneficiary of a dirty deed,
no estate or heirloom
passed to therein,
only an unspeakable act.
Quiet tears seep
from a small and tiny leak,
fragile vase
You will not break this girl.

Though there are many of us
young girls and young boys,
behind altars, pulpits, and in sacristies,
houses of the Holy!
Churches, cathedrals,
even blessed Rome.
They will demand us to keep quiet
of the deplorable, dastardly things
they have done
How must it be, I wonder then
to look in the mirror
and staring back at them
grotesque and unsightly
disfigurements, contortions
mutilated and mangled
- *all mingled-*
evil hearts, eyes and souls?

Hideous antagonists
be damned
in this nonfiction book
the lone snipers and rangers,
solitary wolves roaming among us
not banded or branded
to any organized group or gang.

Still, so effective
at executing
these appalling,
abominable,
loathsome acts,
crossing enemy lines
not once, but countless times,
violating and breaching barriers

traversing forbidden fields
trampling boundaries
in our very private territories.

You must take me for a fool
that, or take me for nothing at all,
or believe I am not human,
a thinking, feeling being
of intelligences of heart and mind,
and perhaps you ask for forgiveness
during your five minutes of penance—
vicars in vespers
purging your guilt
attempting to erase
atrocities and acts
of the highest offense
despicable perpetrator,
having raped and seized;
a child's heart bleeds.

I, regrettable trustee
with a memory,
you have left no legacy,
nothing to redeem
or remember,
no one speaks your name.
Gone.

I have a story to tell
and the child I once was,
robbed of any innocence;
we are all born pure,
brilliant, and bright

the world is out to dim our light
We mustn't let it.

My tears are for
the injured, the wounded,
the war-torn warriors,
the courageous survivors,
the children affected
with pains inflicted,
their shame, a bandage,
wrapped neatly, intact,
protected.

So don't be silent, child,
but speak
of what you've suffered
and endured.
Do not succumb,
they have not won.

Child, be silent no more.

CHAPTER 15

THE RABBIT HOLE
NAVIGATING AND SURVIVING
CHILD SEXUAL ABUSE TRAUMA

Anne Hoyer, Administrator of Legislative and Special Projects for
the Maryland Secretary of State

MY STORY

A bone-chilling scream woke me once again. "Mommy, Mommy, he is going
to climb through the window and put knives in my choo choo!" I tried to
console her as she violently rocked back and forth scratching her skin and
leaving her pajamas blood-soaked. The anger and rage were ignited in me
once again. *My baby, my three-year-old, was traumatized.*

Looking back and through how "it" happened, I wondered. *Would
things have been different if I hadn't lost my mother in February 1997?*

That day I could barely feel any life left in me. I struggled to hold back
tears as I watched the flakes of snow blanket the casket covering the fresh
roses. The sound of the trumpet in the distance, playing Amazing Grace,
haunted me. I did not want to face the end of what I knew and loved, what
I relied on, what made me feel safe. *How would I go on?* Doing it alone
without her was inconceivable. This was the start of my journey spiraling
down "the rabbit hole."

Following my mother's death, I met a man eight months later. I was twenty-five, and he was ten years older. He was charming, funny, talented, and smart, as well as married with two young children. However, I was open to being his friend, as I was desperate to feel alive again. The admiration he had for me made me feel special. All reality blinded me, and I screamed vulnerability which he heard as an opportunity. We grew closer, and eventually, he left his family home and shortly after that was living in mine. I then became his wife and the mother of his daughter in 2002.

Almost a year after the birth of my girl, it was confirmed. My husband's betrayal and obsession with prostitutes were finally uncovered. I was exhausted and beaten down. Caring for a newborn and playing Nancy Drew while doubting myself brought a new and insidious meaning to my life. It was time to get out.

Now living alone as a single mom, I was challenged but determined to make it. I accepted that my daughter's father was "messed up" and lied to me, but I wanted him to be a father to her nonetheless, until the visit that shattered our world.

My daughter was three at this point, and this was the start to the end of her regular visits. "You are going to the movies with Daddy; he will be here to pick you up soon," I said. Suddenly her big blue eyes became dark and hollow as she wailed and kicked and screamed. I asked, "What is going on, sweetie? What is wrong?" She shouted at me as if I weren't sitting right next to her, "Don't ask me, Mommy!" while clenching her fists. I froze with fear and anxiety and spent that weekend pacing and crying. *OMG, what is happening?* I thought.

That Sunday, my anticipation was at its highest, waiting for the return of my little girl. As I heard his truck pulling down my driveway, I sighed with relief and maybe even cried a little. *She was home, thank God.* I welcomed him to keep the peace and make the transition as smooth as possible. He always wanted me to engage him, and he begged for my affection anytime he got the opportunity.

Later that evening, my daughter was restless and needed a diaper change. Her vagina was red, like a rug burn, and she was irritated. What came next rocked my world. She put her fingers in her and said, "Daddy tickles me." I lost my breath and was frozen with fear. *What do I do? Whom do I call?* My aunt came to mind—a child sexual abuse survivor. *Was I going crazy? How do I interpret what my child just said?* I explained to my aunt what I was trying to process, and her response was, "You know what you must do. Call the authorities."

That next morning, I made the call. As I waited to hear back for an appointment, I took my daughter to her pediatrician. I explained my suspicion to the doctor, considering what my daughter told me, and asked her to swab her irritated skin. The answer was no. "She has eczema; that is what you are seeing," she said sternly. I was shocked she wouldn't entertain the information I provided. I left feeling even more alone and frustrated than when I arrived. This was just the beginning of my challenges when searching for answers and support.

A few days later, my three-year-old was alone in a room being interviewed as a uniformed police officer stood by. The sterile, white-walled room intimidated her as she entered hand-in-hand with a stranger. She called out my name, pleading for me to come along. It seemed like an eternity until we were finally reunited. The detective looked at me and said, "You can go home. She didn't disclose any abuse." *Now what? What am I supposed to do? Who do I turn to for answers?* I spent the rest of that afternoon calling therapists who could help us. Phone call after phone call, the same question was presented to me, "Will you be in court with your ex in a possible custody case?" I assumed I would, eventually, because I believed my daughter and was determined not to let anyone hurt her, including her father. Unfortunately, that answer came at a high price. No one was willing to help if they thought there might be a future custody issue. Until the day I spoke with Sally. She was very matter-of-fact and confident in her abilities to treat abused children. I recalled what I was told and shared with her the behaviors (such as night terrors) my daughter was demonstrating. Without hesitation, she agreed to see us.

Therapy began, and I made it clear to my husband that all visits with our daughter would cease due to this new revelation. Not long after, I received divorce papers, including suing me for full, sole, legal custody. I quickly retained an attorney who believed in me, and I was on my way to falling deeper into the "rabbit hole."

The litigation began, and the allegations of child sexual abuse were at the forefront. Those next months were spent doing paperwork, participating in mandatory drug testing, being evaluated, meeting with my daughter's attorney, and attending therapy visits, all while caring for a traumatized child and making a living. I was terrified, scared I would lose my child and/or send her to visit with an abuser. I can recall the first time I had to testify. The judge asked me, "Ms. Hoyer, can you recall an example of an incident that would make you believe your daughter has been abused?" My heart began to flutter, and my hands shook as I replied, "May I stand?" She granted my request. I stood, grabbed the underneath of my breast, and motioned with my tongue as if licking my nipple. "This is what my daughter did. I asked her why and she replied, Daddy showed me how."

The judge issued supervised visitation for my daughter and her father. Those days that followed were hell. Night after night, the terror continued. I felt as if we were in a horror movie. And then, relief. The nightmare ended (in court, that is) after almost eight months, a hundred grand later, and a "no show" from her father. The judge ruled, "Ms. Hoyer, you have full, sole, legal custody and can go where you please." I felt numb with relief that my child was now safe.

My daughter and I moved out of state close to family in search of a new beginning. We settled in and got comfortable. Until the day I met him.

My then almost five-year-old daughter was home with a babysitter, and I was getting a much-needed break. The water was beautiful, and I was enjoying just being Anne (not Mommy) sipping my wine and having adult time with my aunt and uncle on their boat. Nora Jones was playing *"Come away with me."* The water was like glass, and the sun on my skin was just enough to balance the breeze coming off the waterway. It was perfect, and I wanted more time. I ended up at the local restaurant sitting alone at the bar. And it wasn't long until a man sent me a drink. Initially, I was hesitant about his advances but found myself engaged in conversation soon thereafter.

Those next weeks were filled with phone calls and visits from him. It was welcomed since I spent most of my time caring for my daughter both physically and mentally. The distraction from my daily life as a single mom felt good, and it was nice to feel wanted again. We also shared that we were divorced parents with daughters who happened to be close in age. Eventually, we scheduled playdates and talked about moving in together. And that is what we did.

I was caught up in this new relationship's routine but wasn't convinced it was "love or even an equal match." However, I overlooked these differences and was satisfied with the companionship. I know now I was just going through the motions. His parents weren't crazy about us being together either, and it showed. They treated my daughter and me as if we were a nuisance, and for some reason, I accepted it. *Crazy how that sounds to me now, almost 14 years later.* However, they were enamored by their son dating a politician's daughter. Being from a small town up north, they jumped at the chance to be a part of what they considered "high status" and were thrilled to enjoy the benefits, such as attending the Inauguration and the ball with our family.

Little by little, our life became filled with confusion. His daughter was angry and started acting out, including mistreating mine. Her temper tantrums became unbearable, and his eagerness to please her every demand was perplexing. Eventually, we had no choice but to include his ex in the conversation. This was when things started to unravel, and eventually, the truth came out.

"If Daddy was ever to do something bad to me, where would I go?" his daughter asked. I immediately responded, "He will never do anything bad to you." She became agitated and repeated the question. Then I replied, "If that would ever happen, you can be with me." My answer seemed to satisfy her, but I spent the next few hours trying to make sense of this.

As time moved on, my daughter's night terrors were back in full swing, and the chaos in our house became the norm. I met with my boyfriend's ex-wife, who disclosed that her daughter had chronic yeast infections when she was a baby. She suspected that her then-husband (my boyfriend) was possibly to blame. I could not swallow this. *Could this be happening again? Why didn't this woman tell me this before?*

Needing to get away, my daughter and I went to stay at my family home for a few days. That's when my girl told me that this man we were living with was touching his daughter and making her watch. I was speechless and couldn't imagine what would be uncovered next. Outraged, I made the call and confronted him, "I know what you're doing to your daughter and what you're doing to mine!" He paused, and his next words are embedded in my mind forever. He said, "I don't know why I do the fucked-up things I do; it's just how my fucked-up brain works."

As you can imagine, my world was completely turned upside down. However, I regrouped, kicked him out of the house, and returned home. From that point, I immediately enrolled my now-seven-year-old in therapy at Duke. The fantastic therapist uncovered the horrific truth of rape, violence, and abuse. She was forced to call child protective services and they decided to open an investigation. Within days, they closed the case, pointed fingers at me, and said, "this is about your daughter, and you are transferring what her father did onto this new man."

My healing journey began when I accepted that the system was broken and that I couldn't change what had happened. I recognized the most important thing I could do was help my daughter and myself. I did that by moving, finding a stable job, keeping her in therapy, and, most importantly, loving her through it.

THE PRACTICE

Dear Alice,

I know it feels cold and dark down in the "rabbit hole." It's like a fun house full of mirrors, with every corner resulting in a dead end. I'm sure your search for a way out feels aimless, but you must understand there are those who can throw you a lifeline. You need to find them no matter how tired you become. Believe in yourself and put one foot in front of the other. It's okay to have self-doubt and break down, but don't let them see you at your worst. They'll use it against you. I assure you, getting out isn't impossible, though it will take your strength to stay on course.

Please learn from me and know your worth. Understand these predators prey on the vulnerability of kind people who are in a bad place. They disguise themselves as being the "savior." This is where I found myself when my mother passed and then met two abusers who molested my child. Knowing what I know now, I would have avoided a married man. A bad start usually results in a bad or horrific ending. Unfortunately, I was in a dark place and didn't see the hole because I hadn't healed. I was lacking in confidence and self-worth.

Let me be clear, I certainly do not own responsibility for the perpetrator's actions, nor should you. Because even in the best of circumstances, you can find yourself in a bad situation. But my lesson to you is to try and avoid making life-altering decisions when your life seems upside down. It's difficult to see straight when you've been turned around. Take care of yourself when you're in a vulnerable place, and avoid those who manipulate you.

Anyone one of us can find ourselves in this hole and some cases, more than once, like me. I'm living proof lightning can, and does, strike twice. No one is immune to this evil. It affects people of all races, colors, and statuses. Trust your instincts and know you're not alone in your fight to find a way out.

After years of struggling and healing, I built a life back for my family when I thought it was impossible. I moved past the turmoil when I thought I couldn't get out of bed. I value myself and expect that of others. It's possible to do what you set your mind to. For example, I never thought I'd be the catalyst that would prompt a change in legislation to address abuse. Through my position with the state and continued advocacy, I'm now helping others in a way I never knew I could. I pray I've helped you too. I know when you're ready, your story will help others as well.

Perseverance and self-awareness have been my compass. They have led my daughter and me out of the hole. We're now living instead of just surviving. I have moved on, and I want the same for you, my friend.

Never stop searching for the way out.

Keep the Faith,

Alice aka Anne

Anne Hoyer has been an advocate on behalf of families experiencing sexual and domestic abuse trauma since 2006 following her case. She connected with multiple organizations to help bolster awareness of these issues' complexities and their effects on families. In doing so, she has been a speaker at various venues and participated in interviews.

Hired by the Maryland Secretary of State in March 2014 as the coordinator for the Safe at Home/Address Confidentiality Program (ACP), Ms. Hoyer gave eight years of focused dedication and commitment to developing the program. During this time, Ms. Hoyer was an advisor to the Human Trafficking Task Force and was an appointed member by the Governor to sit on the Deed Shielding Task Force and the Workgroup to Address Allegations of Child Abuse and Domestic Violence in Family Court Proceedings. She spearheaded legislative efforts as a result of her participation and testified for reform. These include SB578 and SB17, both of which were successfully passed through the Maryland Legislature.

Under her leadership as the Director of the ACP, two MOUs with the Mexican Embassy and the El Salvadorian Embassy were signed. She has received two Governor Citations, leadership, and unsung heroine awards from Child Justice, which she has been a board member of since January 2014. A National Association of Secretaries of State was also awarded to her in recognition of outstanding service to Maryland in the protection of domestic violence and Human Trafficking victims.

Ms. Hoyer is currently the Administrator of Policy and Special Projects for the Maryland Secretary of State's Office, a Board member of the Child Justice Act Committee, and Board Vice Chair for Child Justice, Inc.

Anne.hoyer@maryland.gov

CHAPTER 16

FINDING COURAGE

FIGHTING TO SPEAK THE TRUTH

Alicia A.G. Limtiaco, Esq.

MY STORY

I sit here contemplating the question, "What is my story?" I find it difficult to answer because my role has always been "the professional," and confronting my self-concept and awareness is a genuinely vulnerable feeling. I understand intellectually, however, that this is essential if I hope to contribute positively to helping victims and survivors of sexual abuse.

I pause and think back to the time of my prosecutor days. I see visions of the all-too-many faces of children. It isn't easy to describe them in any one way. Some were with solemn eyes, blank stares, sometimes looking down so as not to make eye contact. I hear the softness and quivering in their voices. "Why am I here?" "What is this place?" "Am I in trouble?" "Do I have to tell?" Others with confidence about them, sitting up straight, talkative, strong-willed, and even defiant. Family and, at times, close friends of the family were with the children, sitting in the reception area, waiting to be called.

The fear and anxiety of "not knowing" experienced by the victims and families and further complicated by a system that is intimidating, impersonal, and mysterious to many, is like being thrown into a "black hole," into a state of consciousness so surreal with so many questions about how and why "this could have happened?" And like an explosion that hits with so much force you cannot breathe, the discovery that the perpetrator is a family member, or someone known to the family, is overwhelming. Feelings of utter disbelief, rage, and deep despair take over.

Every child has a truth to tell. They may cry, get mad, hit, scream, giggle, and laugh–all a part of their unique being and ways of expression as they find the courage and fight to speak the truth, to tell about what happened.

I am a stranger to whom the most secretive and painful experiences will be told. How can I help to ease the pain? I know building trust is critical and takes time. I understand that gaining trust cannot be underestimated. It's essential to help the children feel safe and disclose the abuse. I also know the trust these children once had in someone who was supposed to be their protector and who has hurt them so severely is now forever broken.

I am asked, "How did these cases impact you?"

There is a natural and gut-wrenching instinct to want to protect and fight for the child and the family. Prosecutors are reminded to ensure we have boundaries and to pay attention to our health issues, including the impact of our work on our mental, emotional, and physical health.

The personal impact is sometimes felt even before you realize it. We are all human, and feelings of sadness are real. I remember early in my career as a prosecutor, receiving support and encouragement from health professionals who also provided treatment and services to abuse victims and survivors. They reminded me about the importance of self-care and the care of others I supervised handling these cases. Whether they referred to possible secondary PTSD and related feelings, given the day-to-day demands of the work, it was necessary to remember that we empathize, unconsciously or consciously, to some degree, which can take a toll on our health. We need then to ensure that we address our feelings, decompress, and reenergize to continue to advocate for and raise the voices of victims and survivors of sexual abuse.

And then there is always the question, *could I have done more to help this child and family? Did I do everything in my power to ensure that no future abuse or harm would come to this child? Are there any other children in the home who may be victimized?* I sit and wonder, at times, how they're doing. *Are they happy? Do they have a family of their own? Are they doing well in their healing process?* I hope they are thriving and surrounded by the love and support they deserve.

THE PRACTICE

We must support and respond to the needs of our most vulnerable and hold offenders accountable. As a prosecutor, I worked with victims and survivors of crime, especially those considered the most vulnerable populations–our children, our elderly, women, and persons with disabilities.

I spent long hours and saw the tears, fears, and courage of many of our children who were victims of sexual abuse. I understand the importance of being committed to justice and being a voice and advocate for children and their families. They are not "just cases;" the lives of human beings are involved and profoundly affected. And our criminal justice system, including prosecution, has a critical role in ensuring that justice is served for all people.

My experience and work with victims and survivors and the criminal justice system also reinforced my belief in the resiliency of the human spirit to overcome even the worst circumstances. Community partners must come together and collaborate when addressing safety and security in our society and provide for and respond to the needs of victims, survivors, and their families.

My interactions with victims who suffered the trauma and pain associated with their victimization revealed the harsh realities of their experiences in trying to understand "the system" and accessing primary health care services such as therapy and counseling, especially when health insurance is not an option. Like our justice system, there is a critical need for our healthcare system to do more to assist our disadvantaged and the underserved.

The saying that information is power is *empowering* for victims and survivors facing and braving "the system." The fear of the unknown is sometimes more intense and overwhelming than what reality reveals and holds. Some questions may be helpful, especially for those who don't have family or friends as lawyers or in the legal profession, in preparing for what will be, as in many cases, a long and complicated journey through "the system."

At the onset, it's crucial to emphasize listening to the victim without judging, to confront and stop any victim blaming, and to let the victim know the abuse is not the victim's fault and that no one deserves to be abused.

Although the particular language in these questions may not be familiar to the general public, they should be and are known to those whose profession and vocation are dedicated to helping sexual abuse victims and survivors. Although they may seem difficult or complex questions to ask, they speak to best- and evidenced-based practices in responding effectively and compassionately to victims of child sexual abuse. According to the National Association of Social Workers, evidence-based practice is "a process in which the practitioner combines well-researched interventions with clinical experience, ethics, client preferences, and culture to guide and inform the delivery of treatments and services."

Here are some of the questions:

- How does the legal and criminal justice system work?
  - Who are the people, agencies, and organizations involved?
  - What are their roles and responsibilities, including law enforcement, prosecutor, investigator, victim advocate, and the court?

- Does the criminal justice process involve and use a "multi-disciplinary team approach" to respond to child sexual abuse?
  - Is the criminal justice process "victim-centered," "trauma-informed," "culturally and linguistically competent," and "gender inclusive"?

- Are the prosecutor, investigator, and victim advocate trained to handle child sexual abuse cases?
  - What specialized training have they received in investigating, prosecuting, and preventing child sexual abuse?

- What kind of victim assistance, preparation, and support will my child receive for the criminal proceedings, including any trial that may be held?

- ○ Will a victim advocate or other support person be allowed to accompany my child during the proceeding to provide moral and emotional support and to confer with my child but not provide legal advice or legal guidance?

- ○ Will the hearing be held in a less aggressive setting than the traditional courtroom, such as reconfiguring the courtroom to be more child-friendly or holding the hearing in the judge's chambers?

- ○ Will a request be made for the judge and court personnel to familiarize my child with a courtroom orientation and explain court procedures to my child?

- Can my child testify and be examined by closed-circuit television, videotape, or audiotape so my child does not have to experience the fear of being face-to-face and testifying in the same room as the defendant?

  - ○ Under what circumstances will the court grant my child's closed circuit, videotaped, or audiotaped testimony?

- Will there be spoken and sign language interpreters available?

  - ○ Will there be assistive technology for deaf and hard-of-hearing persons?

- What is the crime victims' bill of rights or the crime victims' rights act?

- What is the crime victims' compensation program or crime victims' compensation act?

  - ○ Will compensation for damages and restitution for any expenses my child has incurred be part of the criminal case?

- Will the prosecution notify the victim and family of the status of the criminal case and the defendant?

  - ○ Will this include notification of the charges filed against the defendant, changes in custody of the defendant, all court dates, including the defendant's arraignment, pleading to the charges, trial date, sentencing date, and dates of parole board hearings held for the defendant?

○ If the defendant is released before the trial date, will there be a request for appropriate conditions of release such as protective, stay away, and no contact orders, and orders prohibiting threats to commit further abuse?

- Will the prosecution notify or consult with the victim and family on the case disposition, including case dismissal, the defendant's release, a negotiated plea agreement, and the defendant's participation in a pre-trial diversion or pre-trial intervention program?

  ○ Will the victim and family be able to provide a victim impact statement in writing or through oral testimony if there is a negotiated plea agreement and sentencing of the defendant?

  ○ If the case is going to be dismissed, will the prosecutor discuss with the victim and family the reasons for the dismissal?

  ○ Will the victim and family be given an opportunity to provide their input before the dismissal of the case?

- Will assistance be provided regarding the victim's access to treatment, therapy and counseling, support groups, and other services, including public assistance, housing, financial assistance, and transportation, among others?

  ○ Is there a resource handbook with legal, medical, mental health, public health, social services, financial assistance, and other referral resources related to sexual abuse?

  ○ Are there resources for legal issues related to family law, immigration, and labor?

  ○ Are there attorneys, including those willing to provide pro bono services, familiar with sexual abuse legal issues?

Additionally, here are some perspectives on critical issues relating to child sexual abuse. When we refer to a victim-centered approach, we're talking about an approach to care and advocacy founded upon the commitment to address and respond to the needs and concerns of sexual abuse victims with compassion, sensitivity, and respect. It's about providing services and information to victims nonjudgmentally to inform and support their decision-making. A victim-centered approach includes respecting the right of adult victims who do not want to report to law enforcement but seek advocacy, medical treatment, and other support services. Although it may seem counter-intuitive to others for a person not to report the abuse, it's essential to respect the right of adult victims and their decision-making as they are part of their empowerment and healing. It's critical to distinguish this from the mandated reporting requirement involving child victims of sexual abuse. Reporting the sexual abuse of children is not discretionary, and child sexual abuse must and shall be reported to law enforcement authorities.

Law enforcement, prosecutors, and investigators undergo training to help them to understand the dynamics of child sexual abuse and that building rapport and trust with a child is critical so that the child feels safe to disclose the abuse. They're reminded to be patient as this is a process that takes time, and to fight against their instinct to immediately jump into the "what happened?" line of questioning. This is not a TV crime episode that will be investigated, solved, holding a trial, and closing a case in 30 minutes. In real life, the criminal justice process takes time, sometimes months and even years.

Our legal system and prosecution have essential roles in pursuing and achieving justice for victims and their families. However, I've come to understand that it's not the "end all" or "ultimate" closure or resolution of one's victimization but a small piece of a life-long journey and continuum of care and healing with different paths along the way. In other words, although prosecution can provide a sense of closure and even be a form of healing for some victims and their families, there are other profound care and healing approaches more meaningful to a person's health, resilience, and thriving that should and must be encouraged and supported.

This chapter would not be complete without acknowledging the need to prevent child sexual abuse through public awareness and outreach efforts. These efforts incorporate a multi-disciplinary and multi-sectoral approach, including creating task forces and coalitions consisting of survivors of sexual abuse, law enforcement, prosecution, victim service providers, social services, medical, mental, and public health professionals, faith-based organizations, educational institutions, and other community stakeholders. They provide a forum for governmental and non-governmental organizations to establish professional relationships and partnerships and to engage in collaborative domestic and international efforts and strategies to prevent child sexual abuse and to prosecute and hold offenders accountable for these heinous crimes.

RESOURCES

VictimLaw is a searchable database of victims' rights legal provisions, including federal, state, and territorial statutes, tribal laws, state constitutional amendments, court rules, administrative code provisions, and summaries of related court decisions and attorney general opinions: https://victimlaw.org/victimlaw/

Office for Victims of Crime (OVC), one of six Program Offices within the Office of Justice Programs, U.S. Department of Justice: https://ovc.ojp.gov/about

Alicia A. G. Limtiaco, Esq., served as the Director of Policy, Planning, and Community Relations, Lead Litigation Counsel, and Acting Administrator of Court Programs for the Judiciary of Guam, and as Regulation Counsel with the Supreme Court of Guam.

Ms. Limtiaco served as the U.S. Attorney for the Districts of Guam and the Northern Mariana Islands (2010-2017) and as the elected Attorney General of Guam (2007-2010), Acting Chief Prosecutor, and Criminal Sexual Conduct and Family Violence Supervising/Lead Attorney with the Office of the Attorney General. She was a member of the Attorney General's Advisory Committee's (AGAC) working groups/subcommittees, the Co-Chair of the National Association of Attorneys General (NAAG) Criminal Law Committee and the NAAG Youth Access to Alcohol Committee, and the Second Vice Chair of the Conference of Western Attorneys General (CWAG) Executive Team. She established and chaired multi-disciplinary and multi-sectoral coalitions and task forces addressing human trafficking, sexual assault, family violence, child sexual exploitation, drug trafficking, national security, civil rights, cybersecurity, financial crimes, gambling and gaming, reentry, community policing, and public school system health and safety.

Ms. Limtiaco was an associate and a partner in private law firms, and an Assistant Professor and adjunct faculty with the University of Guam and Guam Community College.

Ms. Limtiaco has collaborated with government, civil society, and private sector stakeholders and served as a Pacific Region Focal Point, trainer, speaker, fellow, and consultant on human rights and social and economic justice issues impacting the Pacific Region in educational, political, and community forums at the local, national, regional, and international levels.

Ms. Limtiaco received her undergraduate degree from the University of Southern California and her law degree from the UCLA School of Law. She has over 30 years of legal experience.

CHAPTER 17

THE EMBODIED PATH TO TRUTH

HEALING WITH MINDFUL, EMPOWERING QUESTIONS

Tambry Harris, MA Psy., Cert. Coach and Spiritual Guide

Don't be fooled by me.
Don't be fooled by the face I wear for I wear a mask, a thousand masks,
masks that I'm afraid to take off, and none of them is me.
Pretending is an art that's second nature with me,
but don't be fooled, for God's sake don't be fooled.
I give you the impression that I'm secure,
that all is sunny and unruffled with me, within as well as without,
that confidence is my name and coolness my game,
that the water's calm and I'm in command
and that I need no one, but don't believe me…

Charles C. Finn

MY STORY

It took me three decades to figure out that I wore a mask. I believed the persona I unconsciously created to survive the horrible truth buried deep within me. It took my body screaming loudly to unlock the truth, to let down the mask.

I was a woman wrapped in the image of having it all together with a successful career, a beautiful daughter, and a seemingly happy marriage. I spent years building my résumé and my reputation with degrees, certifications, prestigious jobs, and cultivated exterior. That was until my awakening, a wake-up call that my perfect life was not as I thought it to be.

AWAKENING

The day started like every other business day. My family carpooled, and my husband dropped me off at my building and proceeded to take our daughter to preschool. I'd be attending a workshop about energy and the impact it can have on people. As a lifelong learner, I looked forward to expanding my knowledge. Little did I know how much awareness I'd gain in a single day.

The classroom was set up with tables lined in two rows with two people per table. During the instruction, the facilitator asked for a brave volunteer. A colleague and friend of mine came forward. The facilitator asked Jaslyn to raise her arm out to the side. As they pushed on it, it gave way a little. Next, the facilitator asked the class participants to send Jaslyn positive energy. We did, and her arm seemed incredibly strong as the facilitator pushed on it. Finally, the facilitator asked us to send Jaslyn negative energy. *Why does the energy feel like it comes to me? It feels terrible; I'm just going to observe.* When the facilitator went to push on her arm this time, it quickly fell to her side. As Jaslyn's eyes widened in shock, my body reacted.

Something weird is going on! I can't breathe. My head is swimming. My chest is tight. All I want to do is run out of the room. Is this what a panic attack feels like? Keep breathing. You don't want to draw attention to yourself. See if you can find a safe person. Whom can I trust with this incredibly scary experience? Ah, let me talk to Shelley.

Somehow, I stayed seated until the break. I rushed over to Shelley and pulled her to a quiet corner. Words spilled out of my mouth, "Something strange just happened, and I need someone to process it with me. My body is reacting to the demonstration. I have never experienced anything like this." I breathlessly sought to relay the specifics.

Please don't think I am crazy. Please believe this is real; I need an ally right now.

Shelley listened, believed me, and shared she had something similar happen to her. She encouraged me to explore what was underneath my shocking reaction.

EXPLORING

My mind created my mode of survival for thirty years. Now my body insisted on being heard. *I don't know how this goes, and I need a therapist who can help my body be my pathway to truth. My body is speaking loudly, and I need to listen.*

Years of peeling back the painful layers revealed what I had suppressed for decades; I was a victim of childhood sexual abuse. The awareness started with dreams and then faint memories of places and feelings. I began to remember the dark stairway to the dank basement. I saw myself as a little girl perched on the stool, knowing she couldn't get down. When my therapist asked me what my body wanted to do, my feet started running in little girl steps. *Ah, my little girl wanted to run away. She was trapped, and she knew she didn't dare disobey. When the violation happened, she learned how to emotionally disconnect and leave her body.*

As memories slowly emerged, I found myself rocking back and forth in the chair, both in confirmation of the truth and consoling myself. *I have done this all my life; I have been the one to rock myself, to comfort myself, such a sad reality for a five-year-old child.*

I had to learn to trust my body when I doubted myself and my memories. *Am I making it all up? Did it happen? What is the reality?* The dark story began unfolding underneath the sterile mask created to protect and survive. I can assure you my body told me loudly to believe the dark story. My therapist said a part of me was still trying to protect me from the truth, a truth too painful to handle as a child. That was why I couldn't tap into the memories for years.

Did anyone know what was going on? Why did no one come to my aid? I guess there were more important things for my family. I guess I'm not worthy of their attention or concern. **Is this where my core belief that I'm not worthy came from?**

Pause, breathe.

Unworthiness. This is seemingly a universal feeling for victims of abuse.

Why are we the ones who feel unworthy? Why are we the ones left with the shame? Is it because of what we were told? How we were manipulated into silence? Who are we protecting?

CLAIMING

Claiming my truth took another ten years. *How can I reconcile the constructed story of who my perpetrator was with what he did to me? He was loved by my loved ones. He was friends with Rev. Billy Graham. He was an elder in the church. And he was—a child molester.*

In therapy, my brain would reject surfacing awareness, but my body knew what was real. Sometimes a guttural growl would emerge from my throat, reclaiming a voice silenced for so long. Other times my body would lunge forward, seeking to flee after it had been forced to freeze decades before. I vulnerably worked through the rigid shell I created for protection. The only way to address my woundedness was to let my body do the healing and reconcile the truth.

What is part of the mask, and what is truth? As a way to survive as a child, I tried to be perfect and helpful to not burden a family already filled with pain and heartache. The mask I created to prove my worth was: I am strong. I must strive to achieve. I must suppress my own needs.

How do I release the mask, which has been like protective armor for me? How do I tap into the buried truth: I am worthy. I can have a voice. I am allowed to have needs. Allowing myself to be imperfect and vulnerable can lead me to peace. I can realize my truth and reclaim my life.

Unfortunately, our challenge as survivors is that being vulnerable and claiming our body's wisdom is scary. What will come out if we allow it to speak? Even acknowledging my body's existence was very unnatural for me. When your body is violated at such a young age, it's often shut down and silenced because the pain is so great.

BREATHING

Keep breathing. These are the words that helped me through my panic attack.

Take a deep breath. This thought helped when my head would swim with disbelief, or my body would ache in acknowledgment.

Breathing is something we do voluntarily and involuntarily. It's a gift to help us get in touch with our inner selves and the improved health that comes with each breath.

Breathing deeply and intentionally has helped me navigate my way to truth and brought me into my once impenetrable body.

Learning to be in my body tapped into internal wisdom, which challenged some of those deeply seeded beliefs rooted within me. There's a big difference between mind knowing and body knowing. Our minds can swirl with competing information as well as rationalization. But **our bodies will tell us the truth** when we are still and quiet.

Take a deep, full breath now.

If thoughts have swirled in your head as you have read my story, allow them to settle gently like snowflakes falling to the ground.

Allow yourself to be in your body.

Breathe in, "I am present in my body." Notice what sensations you feel in your body. See if you have a sense of connection to your spirit and soul.

EMBODYING

So fellow survivor, what is the embodied path to truth?

Embodiment is when you're in your body in the present, feel all of its sensations, and have a deep connection to your spirit and soul. For survivors of trauma and abuse, our bodies may not have been safe. We may have had to "go away" when terrible things were done to us. **Through awareness and practice, we can reclaim our bodies for ourselves.**

Embodiment is when we tap into our needs, desires, fears, and wants by listening to our bodies and attending to them. *What, I'm allowed to have needs and desires? I am to honor myself by listening and attending to my body?* Yes, you are!

Embodiment is the ability to recognize and correct cognitive distortions, the lies or manipulated stories we have come to believe, and **allow our bodies to lead us to our inner truth and knowing.** We are worthy of our truth which is a path to freedom and authenticity.

Are you ready to **grow your connection to your body and spirit?**

Are you ready to **claim your inner truth and true value?**

Are you ready to start your **path toward inner freedom and thriving?**

Wonderful! Let's move on to the practices.

THE PRACTICE

What was it like to take a deep breath and imagine all the swirls in your mind and body settling gently like snowflakes to the ground? How was it to rest safely in the stillness?

This is one helpful practice to engage and move into your body. "Practice" is a great word because you have probably practiced other things in your life. Maybe it was a sport or playing a musical instrument where practice allowed you to build skill. With each of these, it took time for it to feel natural for you. I invite you to have fun as you engage your body in an honoring way through this practice.

STEP ONE: CONNECT TO YOUR BODY

To start, find somewhere quiet and comfortable to sit and be still.

- Have your feet firmly planted on the ground. Your knees should be bent, and your head, neck, and shoulders relaxed. Allow your hands to rest gently in your lap, maybe with palms up to signal openness.
- If this is comfortable for you, you can close your eyes, or you can gaze gently at a focal point, maybe a candle.
- Take a deep breath and then slowly exhale. Take two more deep, cleansing breaths.

○ Do a body scan noticing your forehead, jaw, shoulders, back, hips, legs, and feet to notice how just three breaths may have made a difference for you.

Now I invite you to do gentle belly breathing.

○ Place one hand on your upper chest. This hand should remain relatively still as you breathe in and out.

○ The other hand is placed below your ribcage, above your navel. Having a hand here will allow you to feel your diaphragm move as you breathe.

○ Breathe slowly through your nose. The air going into your nose should move downward so that you feel your stomach rise with your hand.

○ The movement (airflow) should be smooth.

○ Exhale slowly.

○ Repeat five times.

Gently notice how you feel after this breathing exercise with your hands touching your chest and stomach. Reflect on how it was to connect to your body in this way.

Now you are ready for your body to speak the truth to you.

STEP TWO: ASK YOURSELF MINDFUL QUESTIONS

Mindfulness allows us to become aware of all the thoughts we carry. We can choose to see them for what they are: our thoughts and not our essence.

As we pay attention to our thoughts and feelings, we can be curious and aware that they exist. We often live in our heads without acknowledging the physical reactions we have in our bodies. We have access to all this information, yet often we have been conditioned to stay in our well-worn patterns of thinking.

Our core thoughts and beliefs will often come into our thinking and decisions without full realization. Being blind to these influences can affect our lives and the lives of others around us. Over time, as we see our mindsets influencing our actions, we learn to claim our power and lessen destructive thoughts and situations.

To understand your core beliefs, we will reflect on messages you heard in your childhood. They may have been said directly or inferred, or your child-mind may have made them up to explain your experiences (like me believing I was unworthy because no one came to my aid).

I invite you to consider the following word stems. On your inhale, breathe in the first word/words offered, and, on your exhale, see what words naturally come out. Allow your inner voice to speak so you can wake up to unhealthy thoughts.

Breathe in, I must...

Breathe out... _____

Continue reflecting on the phrase until no more thoughts or beliefs surface.

For me, it was:
- I must...be concerned for others above myself.
- I must...protect others at all costs.
- I must...have it all together.

Now move on to the next word stem.

Breathe in, NEVER...

Breathe out... _____

For me, it was:
- Never...be lazy or idle.
- Never...rely on anyone.

Breathe in, ALWAYS...

Breathe out... _____

For me, it was:
- Always...be above reproach.
- Always...be there for others.
- Always...stay small, be quiet, and don't stand out.

Sit with your response to these prompts.
- Allow your body to respond to the statements. What do you notice? Any specific feelings?

○ What insights were gained from identifying these beliefs/ thoughts?

○ Summarize the key learnings from this exercise.

Thought Pattern or Belief	Body's Reaction/ Feelings	Insight Gained

Note: If tension, discomfort, or even nausea comes during this exercise, breathe deeply into that space in your body.

STEP THREE: ASK YOURSELF EMPOWERING QUESTIONS

The next level of attention, exploration, and even freedom is to think about the thought patterns and beliefs identified in the earlier exercise and wonder:

○ Where do you come from?

○ What is my body trying to tell me about it?

○ What is my truth?

Write your insights down.

Thought pattern or belief	Where are you from? What are you telling me? What is true?
I must...	
Never...	
Always...	

As you examine your thoughts and beliefs from an objective perspective, what does this do to your feelings or body reactions? Maybe your breathing changes. Perhaps you have less tension in your shoulders. Be curious and just notice.

The more you practice mindfulness, the more you will be able to objectively see what is going on within and around you. You may even experience more peace and energy as you begin to see unhealthy thoughts and beliefs for the lies they are. **I encourage you to empower yourself with your truth.**

STEP FOUR: TAKE ANOTHER EMBODIMENT STEP

Another level of processing is to engage your body in dialogue.

- As questions about your truth emerge, write your question down and then sit to listen to your body's response.

- When you feel like you have heard what your body has to say, write that down as well.

- Is there a next question that comes to you to ask your body? Write that question down.

- Sit and listen for your body's response.

- Continue to do this until you feel like your body is at peace and has been listened to.

At the end of this time, take a deep breath and exhale gratitude. Thank your body for the wisdom it has given you. Thank it for being your partner in truth.

EMBODY YOUR TRUTH

You can claim your inner truth and your path to freedom and thrive.

Once you know and recognize the thoughts and beliefs keeping you stuck, you begin to heal your inner wounds. There are ways to rework the negative thought patterns deeply ingrained within us.

I would love to share the next process step to examine those deeply rooted limiting beliefs and challenge them with healthy, life-giving beliefs that open you up to a whole new chapter in your life. Contact me at tambry@survivorstothrivers.com. I also welcome the opportunity to work with you to claim your exciting next chapter by transforming unhealthy patterns into life-giving ones that manifest your thriver self.

My transformation journey includes removing the mask, seeing the beauty that existed all along, and consciously choosing mindsets that lead to my best self. I hope all survivors will allow their truth to permeate their darkness and guide them along a path to peace, joy, love, and healing.

I leave you with a quote from my book, *Awakening the Light: A Survivors to Thrivers Going-Forward Story,* which shares my healing journey and provides exercises for readers to claim theirs.

"We all have been wounded in some way. What we do with the woundedness defines us. If we learn and grow from our wounds, they can motivate us to claim our Going-Forward Story."

Here's to Thriving! Tambry

Tambry is a leadership/life coach, spiritual guide, author, and speaker who encourages others to manifest their best selves and lives. This involves looking at innate character, personal obstacles, and deepest desires to intentionally embrace their whole selves.

Her twenty years of coaching and nine years of spiritual direction translate into her work with survivors of sexual abuse and domestic violence through the Going Forward: Survivors to Thrivers (GFS2T) organization.

Tambry maximizes her Master's Degree in Applied Psychology and certifications in the areas of Leadership Coaching, Spiritual Direction, Change Management, and Diversity to provide a grounded foundation to serve these beautiful souls. She guides survivors to examine limiting beliefs, find strength in their unique gifts and abilities, and claim a wholehearted, meaningful life.

Tambry's book, *Awakening the Light: A Survivors to Thrivers Going-Forward Story,* was named a 2020 American Book Fest Best Book Finalist. Tambry believes as we make our wounds visible and available, they can serve to heal others. In this workbook, her story of wounding, struggle, and healing encourages survivors to understand their limiting beliefs, examine unhealthy patterns, and claim their going-forward stories.

Tambry created a Group Growth Guide to support small groups wanting to work through the book together.

She released a collaborative book, *How to Heal Our Divides: An Abundance of Opportunities in 2022.*

Books can be purchased at survivorstothrivers.com/buy-the-book.

Tambry was named Mecklenburg Times' 50 Most Influential Women of 2021.

Tambry feeds her spirit enjoying time in nature, live music, and spending time with friends and her soul mate, Randy.

Connect with Tambry:

Website: survivorstothrivers.com or tambryharris.com

Facebook: survivorstothriversofficial

Instagram: survivorstothrivers

LinkedIn: tambry-harris-8a01b0b

CHAPTER 18

HEALING WITH COURAGE

THE DETERMINATION THAT MADE THE PERPETRATOR SURRENDER

Dr. Stanley Beck Banda

MY STORY

"If you do not send the $5000 U.S. in the next 30 minutes, all your family's social media platforms, including your wife's and your sponsor's, will watch you on the nude videos I have of you. Do not try to act clever. We have all the contacts and access to your network."

That came to me as the voice of an online scammer on a WhatsApp voice call. Sadly, I was to find out what it might feel like to be stalked and harassed in a sexual manner. I was able, though, to turn this horrible experience around and use it to better understand the work I do and help others.

While I tried to ask who he was and why he was doing this, he hung up and sent engineered pictures of me nude in compromising positions. *What!?* When I looked at the photos sent to my wife's Facebook page and other Facebook friends' pages, I felt like melting. I felt like that was the end of the world. I lost control of all my social media platforms, and someone with terrible intentions was in control.

Soon after, a woman called me on Messenger and introduced herself as a nurse who had fallen in love with my profile on Facebook. "Hi, Beck. I'm Lucy, a nurse from America. I am single, and I would like to be your friend. Please don't say no because I have never had a relationship with an African man." I responded, "No, I am a married man, I love my wife, and this is not appropriate," and hung up. When I checked her profile, I found out that not only was her message false, but so was she: she only had three friends on Facebook, and two were noted as "from Zambia." I realized this was a continuation of the scam.

I felt confused and horrified. I'm the champion of anti-sexual and gender-based violence in Zambia, the face of the campaign against harassment, and a champion of survivors' healing, protection, and rehabilitation. *How will I stand with my head tall and speak in public once such a lie is broadcasted everywhere?*

One of the institutions my organization partnered with was Grace Cares International, which had just committed the resources to my organization to fight sexual and gender-based violence and take care of the survivors. *What will the partner think about my morals and integrity when they see this posting of me being portrayed as a person involved in online nude activities?*

While I was thinking about all this, I received a video call on WhatsApp from the young lady, and, this time around, she was half naked. "Hi, Stan! I love you! I love you! Please show me what you've got; I want to kiss it," she shouted repeatedly. I hung up and was very distraught. I blocked her and immediately shared with a friend of mine in my office what was happening. I told him I hung up on her and blocked her. Then I called members of staff at the office and shared this distressing information. One of them told me, "Your number is publicly displayed on your Facebook profile, which is a dangerous thing to do." "Oh," I groaned. And thought out loud: "I think this person could be the internet scammer."

A little later that morning, I arrived at my office and we continued to plan for our sexual and gender-based workshop and theatre for community action outreach activities. I worked on the sexual and gender-based violence manual for workplace management teams, immersed in that work since, in my mind, I was convinced the sexual harassment calls were over because I blocked both numbers the calls came in on.

But it wasn't the end. I received another strange WhatsApp video using a different phone number. I was restless, worried, scared, and angry. I thought: *she might be planning to trap me.* Then I shared my fears, worries, and confusion with my staff, letting them know I received another video call with the same language and content as the last and had hung up on her. They already heard me shouting and screaming. And I was soon to find out that before I could switch off the phone, she sent more than ten nude pictures. I panicked and switched off the phone.

"What? She was naked?!" was the response from my wife when I shared with her what happened at the office. Then she asked me why I switched off my phone. I looked into my wife's eyes, and I could see how worried she was and her disappointment and pain. "She is a scammer, and she wants to trap me," I related. I softly asked my beautiful wife to trust me and assured her that I blocked the scammer on both the WhatsApp and Facebook pages. "This is terrible," my wife said. "How can she call you naked and start telling you she loves you just like that?" That night I did not bother to switch on the phone and decided to go to bed early.

The following morning, I left for work and switched on the phone. There was nothing new or strange. I felt relieved. "Thank God this drama has come to an end," I told my staff. I asked about their well-being and then said, "Let's finish the plans that we started working on yesterday," feeling relieved and even a little cheery. But my sentiment was misplaced.

"Jesus Christ!" I exclaimed after opening a WhatsApp message. I found a full display of more nude pictures of me. There were nude pictures placed next to my profile picture with a message: "Don't act clever Dr. Stan—check who we already have contact with. Wait for instructions, and don't play any games. You are a respected person, a Christian, and a leader—you don't want that to change. Follow the instructions."

I went outside the office, highly agitated and confused. Before I could call my wife to explain and get support, a man called me on WhatsApp and gave me the following instructions: "If you do not send the $5,000 in the next 30 minutes, your entire family will be sent nude photos and videos of you. Do not try to act clever. We have all your contacts and access to your network."

$5,000!? How am I going to handle all this? I was terrified but pulled myself together and refused to break down. I took a deep breath and called two staff members to tell them about the continued abuse. With my head down, embarrassed and upset, I said, "Colleagues, I'm in deeper trouble." They asked me what was going on, and I told them I was now being asked for ransom. I could see they all looked very worried and disappointed. I even shared the pictures; I was afraid they wouldn't believe me. They reacted with understandable shock. At that same moment, another call came through on another number but with the same caller saying: "Your 30 minutes are slowly fading. The whole world will soon be reading about you and seeing nude pictures of you. They will mock you, and you will be finished."

Oh my God, my reputation! My projects, my family! I agonized. But I told my staff I would fight back, saying, "Enough is enough. I will face this criminal. I will inform my wife, go to the police and report this number and show them the messages. I will also write a message on my Facebook and distance myself from this horrible person's fake online scam."

And then I did fight back. I called the scammer and challenged him to go ahead and tell the world whatever he wanted to. I told him what he was doing led people to being swindled and to commit suicide. I told him I was ready for him. I then called my wife and the police and posted a Facebook message on my Facebook page.

I received support from almost all my Facebook friends and my beloved wife. My staff encouraged me to report the incident at the police station. "Comrades, don't worry. I will handle this. With your support, I will overcome. I will be back. Let me go to the police and report this matter," I gained courage: *after all, none of this is true!* I also told myself that once I (or anyone) fall and dance to scammers' tunes, it's not only the end of me, but it's also the end of my important work fighting sexual and gender-based violence. I realized that was exactly what was happening!

I knew I needed to be strong and win this. When I reached the police station, I narrated my story, and they encouraged me to be strong. They told me I was the sixth person to report such a case that day.

"Don't worry, Dr. Beck Banda, Sir, you're not the first one to come and report this case," they said. "Give us the number and relax. We shall monitor the activities of this number." While I was in the police station, Facebook sent me a message that they suspected my account was hacked and they wanted to remove my mobile number. They showed me the numbers they uncovered being associated with my account, and I recognized some of them as ones used by the scammer. I began to feel more relieved. I also learned lessons I could apply elsewhere in my work and life. I won!

THE PRACTICE

My core business is to prevent sexual and gender-based violence both online and offline. I therefore told myself: *if I don't break the silence, how can I ask or encourage others to break the silence?* Thankfully, many others were in my camp. "We are with you, Dr. Beck," many Facebook followers wrote on my timeline. I felt like a winner when I had the courage to challenge the horrible online criminal perpetrator-scammer and show him I was ready for him.

I now understand what it feels like to be sexually harassed, threatened, and stigmatized. As a practitioner, counselor, and advocate for anti-sexual and gender-based violence, I appreciate the courage and peer support contributing to timely healing. And how important it is to build those and rely on them. Once you take a moment to think about how much your life, and the lives of other people who look up to you, would be destroyed if you buy into someone's abuse (even a one-off event like the one I experienced), you realize we have to help each other. We cannot break in the face of such things. And we need each other not to.

As a practitioner, I realize breaking the silence is the first step towards self-healing. My experience has helped me gain the skills and knowledge about how to handle online sexual violence and threats that come with dealing with a person you have not met, who you cannot locate, and what people like this are capable of.

Perpetrators win when fear and shame overwhelm you. Fear is one contributing factor to wrong decision-making. Once I found my courage, I understood that social media-based (as well as other types of sexual harassment) perpetrated by heinous individuals could threaten and shame, but as long as we act, their ability to harm can be short-lived. My experience made me a better person who knows how to handle online abuse, but I also better understand why so many perpetrators of other types get away with it for so long.

Now I don't just encourage others to be courageous and break the silence; I share my own real personal experience. This is a clear testimony that overcoming sexual violence and abuse needs a human face from as many as possible. We must come out in the open, break the silence, and share our stories. Many survivors who've lost many years staying in denial need the real-life experience of being supported to share and heal.

Another very important lesson I learned is that people in a relationship must try, by all means, to share with their partners before they open up to other people. Having a support system is critical. This facilitates healing.

My organization YOCUPA 7ASIDE-ASHAGs strongly recognizes the need to find ways and means to fight against sexual violence online and offline. I've emerged as stronger and more determined to help others and those in denial. I stand as a testimony and example of the benefit of breaking the silence, regardless of your social status. My choice to face the challenge and win this online sexual harassment amidst fear, uncertainty, worry, and anxiety helps me better serve others' lives while preventing self-blame and denial and encouraging others to join the fight. I'm a victor today because I refused to let fear dominate my heart. I'm a winner today because I refused to remain silent.

It doesn't matter what the perpetrators use to keep us silent; what matters is we come to learn there is healing and justice in breaking the silence. I decided to wage war against sexual and gender-based violence through an innovation I developed called Youth Cultural Promotion Association (YOCUPA) 7ASIDE-Anti Sexual Harassment Action Groups (ASHAGS). I can and will overcome every obstacle that tries to frustrate my effort to fight sexual and gender-based violence. We must rise and fight sexual abuse and violence at all levels. But more importantly, we must build an army and network of brave survivors for online and on-the-ground battles.

Dr. Beck Stanley Banda is a public health, youth, and community education expert with profound knowledge, skills, and experience cultivated over 30 years in the field. His work has largely focused on helping adolescents, youth, and women in Zambia. Dr. Beck Stanley Banda is the founder and Chief Executive Officer of Youth Cultural Promotion Association (YOCUPA), the innovator of Safe Motherhood Action Groups (SMAGs), one of Zambia's maternal health best practices and YOCUPA 7ASIDE-Anti Sexual Harassment Action Groups (ASHAGs). He is the researcher, author, and practitioner of theatre for community action pedagogy. He is also a team player and a determined and courageous visionary leader. He is a strong believer in bottom-up methods of community and participatory ways of addressing community challenges and a committed advocate of anti-sexual and gender-based violence.

Connect with Dr. Banda:

https://www.facebook.com/beck.banda/

https://www.facebook.com/bwachaconst2021/

https://www.facebook.com/people/7-Aside-ASHAGs/100065671355205/

https://m.facebook.com/Yocupa/

https://www.linkedin.com/today/author/dr-beck-banda-7280ba37

https://twitter.com/banda_beck

https://gracecares.org/project/yocupa-youth-cultural-promotion-association/

CHAPTER 19

BREAKING THE CYCLE
YOU DON'T HAVE TO SELL YOUR SOUL TO HAVE MONEY

Heidi Henyon

MY STORY

2020

"Not again," I said out loud as my body felt like crumbling to the ground. *Oh my God, how did my credit card balances get so high again? I just want to run away.*

It felt like my heart wanted to explode; it was beating so fast. My stomach wrapped tighter than a boa constrictor.

Will I ever break the cycle of money taking over my life? Making money and losing it, making money and losing it! Slipping through my fingers like water.

1964: MY ONLY CHILDHOOD MEMORY

Wailing, deep sobbing, Mother crying out, "He's dead, he is dead." Sister so sad, in tears.

Me: relief floods my little body. I want to dance; a feeling of being safe came over me. *Don't let them know your joy. Lie; show them 'sad.'*

I never knew why I didn't remember stuff other kids did. Like listening to the story of how excited and overjoyed my friend Paul felt when he was six and looked under the Christmas tree to see his new shiny blue bike. I didn't remember getting a bike.

I could listen to the stories my family told of childhood and build a picture of riding a bike, but I never remembered doing it. I only remember what they told me it was like.

2014: THE POEM

The softness of rain,
The gentleness of my spirit,
They are still there.

I respond to kindness from the giving spirits in my life. I'm learning what's safe, what's fun, and what is kind.

Warped by what happened when I was little, so little. Only six.

The moments that should have been safe, fun, kind—warnings of ill
to come.
The innocence of being a child became the magnet of their abuse.

Into oblivion, into the recesses deep in my unconscious, I put the pain,
my memories.
Protecting me the only way I could.
Time will continue, my memories will not.

Why was I so self-destructive as I grew up?
Teenage, young adult, lost but I did not know why.
Why did I not stay with the kindness and good that happened along
the way?

54, adult, the deep recesses opened up, time my little child is
seen, remembered.
Horror, pain, shock, despair,

Anger, depression, betrayal, lost. . .so lost.

Suicide please, quiet please, oblivion. . .please.

No, No, NOOOOO

My child deserves more, I deserve more.

2012: THE MEMORIES COME BACK

Turn right, Turn Right off 66 to 243. My mind screamed. *You can do this.*

Oh God, they're pulling me out of the closet.

Left on 29. Okay, left on 29. I can get to MB's.

Do whatever they say; it will hurt less.

I feel so small in my body as I drive the car. I'm so small; they're so big; I don't know what to do.

Three more miles of sheer hell, memories flooding into my head, my body shaking, and my mind giving me directions:

Left on Prosperity. Oh no, no, no, not yet, left on Cedar. Oh yeah, Cedar. Concentrate; small road, not a highway, thank God. Left on Gallows.

Just a little bit more. There's her office. Left into the parking lot. Parking space right in front. Okay.

The next thing I knew, I was in my counselor's office, and she was talking to me; I was explaining what had happened as I drove to her office. She looked me straight in the eyes, kindness and empathy flooding into every pore of my being.

"I've been waiting for you to remember."

2 HOURS EARLIER

I was visiting with my dad, and out of the blue, he said, "I'm sorry I wasn't there when you were a little girl to keep you safe."

My body started to feel weird, kind of numb. The room around me came into sharp focus. I could hear the clock ticking in the other room, the dog snoring next to my 89-year-old father.

Then his words receded into the background as I drew inward.

"I know your mother was harsh; I didn't understand how bad. I did come back when Tom was murdered and took care of you."

I hear his words but have no idea what's being said. I knew when he was done talking.

"I have to leave. I have an appointment with my counselor," was all that came out. I was frozen inside.

I was numb all over, and my mind was very empty. Then something started to stir inside. I felt the warmth of the seat after it was heated by the sun. I put my key in the ignition. Turn. *Vrooom,* the car started. I drove away.

Over the next 40 minutes, starting very slowly, horrible images began flooding my mind. At first, a slow trickle, like when you remember a violent scene from a movie you saw long ago, distant and not personal.

As the highway sped past, the images became more vivid, more visceral, and very personal. Inside, my body was shaking, and the contents of my stomach were sour, and wanting to leave.

I made it to MB's office.

MB, my counselor, is wonderful. From the behaviors of my past and present challenges, she knew I was sexually abused as a child. Yet she never pushed me to remember. She trusted that they'd surface when I was strong enough and emotionally ready. And boy, did they.

I was very young, and they were very bad. My dad didn't even realize the depth of the abuse. He never even dreamed there was sexual abuse. How could he know my mother sold me out to a sexual predator so she could be safe and financially secure? My parents were divorced, and he was in England.

I spent a few hours with MB that day and the next. She helped me get stable and functioning.

TODAY LOOKING BACK

MB and I used some talk therapy, ceremony, energy work, and journaling. The 2014 poem at the beginning of this chapter came out of the journaling. It took a few months to heal.

This didn't mean the memories were gone or all the triggers or behaviors healed. What it means is they're not driving my life. The unconscious behavior of burying memories helped me survive. I cleverly adapted this strategy to apply to many things in my life, especially money.

The memories gave me an understanding of my drug and alcohol addiction from age ten to 27, why I was incredibly promiscuous, and why I couldn't read above a first-grade level until I was 17.

So much of my life was explained by the memories. I wasn't a bad person, a slut, or a drug addict. I was a child who was severely abused. These "bad and harmful" behaviors were coping mechanisms developed, so I didn't feel the extreme emotional pain deep inside me.

No wonder the only real memory for most of my life was the death of the man who abused me.

Yet they didn't explain why money always slipped through my fingers. At age 54, I still hid my head in the sand regarding finances and didn't realize it.

I had no clue they were even linked until a bit ago.

MY MONEY HISTORY

Age nine: I'd get a quarter allowance, gone in a flash for candy, or when I was so fearful at night, I'd pay my sister to let my little body crawl in her bed to feel safe.

First job at 16: I was a counter girl at Roy Rogers. I was so cool in my shiny black cowboy boots, taking the money in and giving the change out.

Paycheck in my hand cashed and a new batch of drugs and alcohol ready for the week.

Twenty-three, first grown-up job as a computer salesperson: Guess what? Now I had credit and my first credit card. I loved to spend that money. I was in debt way over my head in a year.

Thirty, married, child, great job, lots of money: Gone in a flash, and now more credit cards run to the max, but my cunning mind told me: *you can refinance your house, pay off the cards, and have some left over for home improvement!* Voilá all taken care of.

Thirty-seven, bigger job, lots more money, lots of debt, no more refinancing: My first foray with the possibility of bankruptcy. Fortunately, Consumer Credit was happy to reduce my payments and interest. Even some of the debt was forgiven. The catch: Within a year of showing good behavior, like magic, credit card companies started offering me high-interest, low-balance cards. Now I was disciplined; I could handle it.

Forty-four, back in the same place: Over the last few years, the credit card companies systematically raised my limits, and I fell back into the old patterns until, at 51, I filed for bankruptcy. So much money just slipped through my fingers over the years. Retirement, stock options, inheritance. I learned you could take out low-interest loans against your retirement. Cool, now I was paying myself.

OMG, the stories I told myself!

I took a surface look at my behavior around money. I blamed the system that feeds on our weakness. Then I thought I was smart by blaming my parents for never teaching me about money.

I got into this space one more time and finally realized something much deeper was going on. I studied the unconscious and how we form beliefs we're unaware of.

Early in my career as a transformational coach, I learned a tool called the seven/nine-year cycle. Through his years of coaching, my teacher Ernie Pavan discovered that behavioral patterns tend to follow a seven/nine-year cycle. He developed a tool for us to use with ourselves and clients to take a deep look at these cyclic patterns.

I applied this to relationships and other parts of my life. I applied it to finances and money. That's how I learned the cycle I laid out earlier. And I found some superficial understanding.

Yet, this time felt different. I realized why. I was ready to take my head out of the sand.

This time as I did the seven/nine-year cycle, I felt my body tighten and the nausea rise in my belly. Big drops of water filled my eyes. I heard deep inside: *I hated her so much. She sold me out for money.*

I knew instinctively that was when my little girl, hiding her memories to stay safe, made the unconscious decision that money equaled hate.

No wonder I pushed it away. My conscious mind was stunned. That didn't make sense. But I couldn't deny what my body felt. Every part of me knew this was true. And if money was hate, why would I keep it?

I was so tired after this discovery. I slept for 12 hours straight. As I woke, the room just starting to show a hint of light as the dawn approached; I knew the realization went further: *You have to sell your soul to have money.*

Boom. That was how I unconsciously felt about money all my life.

All because I was used as a sexual toy to a man who promised to care for my mom financially. It's almost too bizarre to comprehend.

Wow. I called my friend Stacy, an amazing coach I met through my training and did deep-yet-quick release work.

NEXT DAY

I go to the mailbox and see what looks like a check from the county. As I open it, to my great surprise, there's an unexpected refund for property taxes I've overpaid since 2018. It's the amount I need to keep my business solvent for a couple of months. I feel water well up in my eyes.

The next day I dove deep into my finances and had absolutely none of the fear or stomachache I normally felt. I felt empowered.

I put together a plan to handle all of it, and it didn't include using more credit, a second mortgage, or borrowing money.

Several papers and studies prove that when we've suffered childhood sexual abuse, we suffer financially. A recent paper published by a health economist at Washington University in Missouri examines the correlation between child sexual abuse victims and their earning potential throughout their lives. According to the report, experiencing sexual trauma in childhood "dramatically increases the likelihood that survivors will struggle financially as adults."

Maybe you're reading this chapter because you're ready to take a deep look at your cycles and money.

In the next section, I take you through the simple yet very powerful process of looking at the patterns and cycles in your life that are still causing problems.

THE PRACTICE

7/9 YEAR CYCLE

How often have you heard yourself saying, "not this again?" or, "I thought I was done with that," as you realize you're repeating a mistake or behavior?

My coach and mentor, Ernie Pavan, put this process together after realizing these large patterns tend to follow a seven- to nine-year cycle. It's one of the best tools I know for figuring out where these patterns come from.

1. Awareness

    Your body remembers every thought, emotion, and physical experience you've had—everything that was said to you, every word you spoke, and every action you've taken. It remembers everything from the beginning of your life!

    These memories are stored at a cellular level. Each of these memories has a belief attached to it. The beliefs get anchored in our unconscious due to traumatic experiences or repeated experiences from others or yourself. Many of these form during early childhood.

    Once a belief is "anchored," a cyclical pattern of events occurs in your life. This is because one of the jobs of the unconscious is to heal our trauma, and it creates these as opportunities for us to heal and learn.

    You stay stuck in this pattern until the root cause/belief becomes conscious and is resolved. Awareness that we have these patterns is the first step.

2. You have to be willing to do the hard work.

    This work is not comfortable. Yet, you're already uncomfortable with the problem, so why not be uncomfortable in the process of finding the root of the problem and the solution?

    Commit yourself to do this process and schedule time for it. The more committed you are, the deeper the transformation will be. Have a journal so you can write the cycles and insights you have.

3. The cycles and patterns

    1. Start with the present year. For example, I'm writing this in 2022. At the top of a piece of paper or page in your journal, write the year and the age you are now. Next, subtract seven from the starting year. Write that year and your age at the time five lines down the page.

        In this example, that will be 2015. If your journal doesn't have lines, leave enough space to write.

    2. Repeat this process until you're at the year of your birth. For example, if you were born in 1990, it looks like this:

        2022 age 32

        2015 age 25

        2008 age18

        2001 age 11

        1994 age 4

        1990 age 0

    3. Take time to reflect on the problem you're examining; what is happening right now? Write that in the 2022 space. When you have emptied your mind and thoughts, go to the next year. Reflect on what was happening at that age.

        Let go and write whatever comes up. Let your unconscious speak to you.

        Repeat this process to birth.

        If you get to where you have no memories. Ask yourself what stories your parents, siblings, and others told you. Ask them. Think of references like what grade you were in.

        You may find your cycle is more like nine years. Adjust the ages and dates accordingly.

    4. What's the pattern?

        Look at your notes. See if any patterns or a-ha moments pop out.

        You may see a false belief you've been running in your head: I'm not good enough. I don't deserve this. I give all my money to my partners. I have to support others. I have to push myself down, so my partner feels good about themselves. I feel guilty when I put myself first.

Trust what you discover. Write your thoughts and feelings about these.

5. Forgiveness

   Forgiveness is the most powerful tool, especially when we can forgive ourselves.

   Write a letter to yourself forgiving yourself for ever having held those beliefs.

   Rewrite the negative beliefs in a positive way and read this to yourself every day for 30 days.

   If you're angry at someone, write a rage letter. Completely empty out the negative feelings. Burn it or tear it up and flush it down the toilet.

6. Give yourself time to integrate these new learnings and feel over the next few days. You may need to repeat this process a few times to get more understanding. Give yourself a few days in between so the learnings and a-ha moments can sink in. You may also want to reach out for help.

Think about this time as sacred. Find a quiet spot where you will not be disturbed. You can light a candle, take a centering breath, and ask your unconscious and higher self to reveal what you need to know now in a gentle, kind, and easy manner.

I have a simple form for this process. You can email me at info@ heidihenyon.com, and I will send it to you and be happy to answer any of your questions.

Become your own best friend during this process. Be kind and gentle to yourself. We were taught not to from our childhood experiences. That was a lie, a belief you no longer have to obey.

Heidi spends her time at her retreat center hosting transformational workshops and providing one-on-one programs where women can safely and quickly heal from trauma and abuse so they can thrive in life.

Drawing on her healing journey and 40-plus years of experience, her clients feel heard and understood and experience profound healing in quick and gentle ways. They learn to be their own best friend and advocate. Many have healed generational wounds, so they are not passed to the next generations.

She received her first certifications in applied kinesiology and behavioral kinesiology when she was 21. She has continued to study energy medicine, movement, the unconscious mind, and the art of ritual and ceremony. While in corporate America, teaching internationally in the computer industry, she continued to study internationally and work privately with clients. Finally, in 2001 she left her corporate position of 25 years, realizing her heart was in helping people to heal from personal and generational trauma and feel whole.

Heidi feels blessed and honored to learn and share with hundreds of clients over the years and to have studied with wonderful teachers like Roselyn Breyer, Hyemeyohsts Storm, Emilie Conrad, Sobonfu Some' and Avalon Empowerment. She studied in the Peruvian Andes and rainforest, Bolivia, Mexico, Europe, Nepal, and the United States.

In addition, she is a master NLP Practitioner, Certified Miracle Minded Coach, certified and licensed massage therapist, movement teacher, health coach, and author of three Amazon bestselling books.

"I believe our greatest teacher is our living body and spirit. The inherent wisdom and joy within let us know exactly what is best for our joy and wholeness if we pay attention and listen deeply."

Connect with Heidi:

www.heidihenyon.com

https://www.facebook.com/heidisthompson

https://calendly.com/heidihenyon/gift-session-from-sacred-spaces-book

CHAPTER 20

FORGIVENESS
PREVENTING THEIR BEHAVIOR FROM DESTROYING MY HEART

Lianne Hofer, CMWC

MY STORY

On the phone that night, I knew. I knew I would be on my own. I was too young to have this library of nauseating memories of being repeatedly molested and raped by my father. On the brink of hysteria, I begged my mother to come home.

Can't she hear the desperation in my voice? My mind demanded.

"Why can't you please come home?" I sobbed the words out.

Her refusal to come home that night and my father's smug smile as he hung up the phone cemented my knowing. No one was coming to save me; it would be up to me to save myself.

The man who should have been my biggest protector, my father, glared a look as a reminder to stay quiet, not to say another word on the phone to my mother. I vowed that once I was old enough, I'd move away, far enough away to never be touched by him again. I knew in those moments it was going to be a long haul. I was only four.

As I grew up, as hard as I tried to stay away from him, I was often alone in his presence. My mother worked nights or weekends, leaving me at his mercy at the time of day I needed someone around the most. He put my siblings to bed and brought me to his. He came into my room, even with a closed door. He lifted my shirt, my skirt, or my pajamas, and grabbed me as a father should not grab his daughter. He gave me magazines and told me to look at them. The shiny pages were filled with naked children and adults. In my head, I tried to make sense of this. It all felt so wrong, and I didn't have the vocabulary to say it. He laid on top of me, pulling my clothes out of the way so he could try to push his penis into areas not made for an adult. Some nights I felt I had left my body to wait for the torture to end. Always in fear in his presence, my body trembled when he negotiated to get me alone.

I was embarrassed because he was my father and embarrassed because my mother was too deep in her own bullshit to notice or help. I was embarrassed because it kept happening, and I couldn't find a way to stop it. One Halloween night was embarrassing in front of someone else. I was in grade school, and like every other kid on Halloween, the anticipation of dressing up in my hand-created costume and going out for candy had me giddy. Patiently waiting to go out after dark, I realized my mistake as we all assembled at the door. I didn't line up a friend to walk with.

My mother took my younger siblings and sent me out with him. Again, alone with him. We proceeded out, stopping at houses. Along the way, there were pockets of kids giggling and having fun. I craved to be in a crowd with my friends giggling. Instead, I walked with him as far ahead as I dared without causing him to call me closer. Arriving near the end of the street, we walked up the last driveway of the night straight to the front door. The woman answered and gave me a candy and a kind smile. She commented on my dad being dressed as a doctor. He commented that he was doing breast checks and pushed his hands forward in a squeezing motion. I was so mortified. I never saw her reaction because I sprinted down the steps with my head down. Fortunately, home was our next and last stop, and everyone was back, comparing their candy loot.

I stayed quiet because I was threatened by his size, his glances, and of course, the nighttime visits. The words he actually uttered have faded, and I'm grateful for that now. Back then, I remember being so afraid that if I said something, the powers that be would take away what I knew and the things that brought me the comfort I clung to. My comfort was my extended family, school, and above all, my friends. What would I have left if these small comforts were ripped away from me? With these "small" comforts, I felt normal for a while. Even at school when the mean girls were, well, mean, the school was safer than home. I could get away from the mean girls. I was experienced in hiding. Being out of our house allowed the fight-or-flight nerves to calm for a small amount of glorious time.

During my teens, being super busy kept me safely away from home. In middle school, I kept busy helping my mom with her in-home party business and always wondered if she realized or thought why her daughter asked to come along, even on weekend gigs. High school allowed a job, sports, study groups, and a driver's license. I dared to think the abuse was over—actually believing it for a while. I was wrong. One night shortly after that thought felt like it had merit, I woke from a dream about my latest crush. At some point, between being asked out and eating pizza, my dream turned steamy—too steamy for a first date. It felt wrong in the dream, astonishingly wrong.

Dates don't happen like this. Teenager dates don't do this! Bellowed from somewhere in my brain.

Trying to shake the heaviness of slumber, I struggled to open my eyes and focus. It was dark, and I saw a shadow next to me on the bed. Then I felt it. It came in short bursts, his hot breath on my cheek filling my ear. I didn't move, my breath catching in my nose as I tried to keep breathing evenly. I wanted to scream and push away. Experience said, *stay still.*

"Just go with it," he murmured.

I wanted to puke.

"Relax into it," he continued, as his hands shifted under the sheets and his fingers explored and pushed between my legs. I was on high alert, considering my options. He pinned me with the covers. My mother was not home. I lay there feeling trapped. He stopped, flashed a half grin, sighed a satisfied exhale, and got up. He straightened his pants and left, closing the door softly behind him.

I curled in a ball that night, crying. Deep sorrowful sobs came from places I didn't know existed. Once the pillow was soaked with my sadness, and the shaking subsided, I attempted to find sleep again. Finding it elusive, I replayed too many painful memories. Somewhere in the replays, the courage surfaced to declare that I was ready to save myself.

At school the next day, the plotting began, slowly at first because I was tired, then escalating in an adrenaline high as ideas formed a plan. Excitement fueled the anticipation for the final bell. I practically flew out of the school building, heading straight home. I was on a mission to get there before everyone else. I had to see if my plan worked.

I hit the top step of the staircase and tore down the hall into my room, slamming the door shut. I stopped, needing a moment to catch my breath. I was curious if I'd sleep soundly tonight and every night that followed. The plan was to rearrange the furniture. Pushing my desk, I was amazed it slid quietly from under the window across the bedroom floor. My lips curled in a huge grin.

No one will hear this, I thought. That desk slid almost silently all the way to the doorway. "This is good," I whispered to myself.

Unfortunately, the desk was too narrow this way, and if the door was pushed hard enough, the desk wouldn't hold its place. I paused, not ready to give up. Feeling defeat attempting to creep in, I sat on the desktop, swinging my feet, determined to make this idea work. Deep in my gut, I knew this was a good plan.

What if I try it sideways? I wondered if I said the thought out loud. Sliding the desk sideways created a perfect fit between the footboard and the door! The door opened less than an inch with no space for peeking.

I let out a small cry of joy.

That night, the desk quietly found its way back to the foot of my bed, turned sideways.

That night just as I was drifting off to peaceful slumber...

Jiggle.

Softly yet a little louder, I heard it again.

Jiggle, bump.

I opened my eyes wide and slammed them shut. Looking at the snapshot of the door behind my eyelids, I saw the door was still closed. I considered exhaling and found my chest wouldn't allow it. My ears hummed as they intently waited for the sounds I ached for. Footsteps walking down the hallway, away from my room. *Had I heard them?* Yes, I definitely heard them.

I wasn't smiling; I was beaming with joy!

I would be sleeping with that desk there tomorrow night and every night too.

My parents had a falling out shortly after that night, and he moved out. The desk returned its nightly stance back under the window. Being able to shift from being on constant hyper-alert was starting to become comfortable.

One of my teachers at school was kind and felt safe to talk with, so I confided in her in a short conversation. By law, teachers have to report abuse. She had to tell the authorities. I took control, and it felt good. In my senior year of school, the authorities and, unfortunately, the local rag newspaper were all involved in my gigantic secret. The secret was out, and my mother was now forced to confront my abuse and react. She sent me to therapy. I quit therapy. I tried again. How have I found healing?

THE PRACTICE

The healing started in the smallest chips. I wasn't ready to rip off the scab that held in the trauma. I was holding it all in tight, afraid somehow of the eruption of searing pain if the scab came off.

Big healing snuck up on me. Good thing it was spontaneous, for I created a strong resistance to letting anyone or anything in; just ask my therapists. The healing that found me is called Reiki, and it removed the scab softly for the clearing and healing to begin.

During a massage appointment, the therapist asked me: "Can I incorporate a healing modality called Reiki." According to The International Center for Reiki Training, Reiki is a Japanese stress reduction and relaxation technique that promotes healing. Curious, I agreed. A flood of ugly cries released like a broken dam, and a box of snot-filled tissues later, it felt like the Reiki cut through my brick fortress wall like a hot knife through soft butter. Reiki cut those walls open and allowed the discharge of the heavy energy I had buried for so long. Reiki busted open a door I didn't know existed and revealed I could safely let the built-up stress and festered feelings go. I felt like a load of bricks was lifted off my soul.

That therapist opened me to spirituality. Knowing I was open to spirituality, a friend invited me to take a Reiki class. I studied each level with enthusiasm and joy, ending my formal training as a Reiki Master and Master Teacher. On my journey, spirituality spoke to me as nothing else had. There are so many teachers and so much wisdom to dive into. The Buddha said, "Holding onto anger is like grasping a hot coal with the intent of throwing it at someone else; you are the one who gets burned." This quote spoke to my very being, showing alternative ways to look at life. I found my relationship with myself deepened. I realized how the world around me is sacred. I found so much more than just the practice of Reiki.

In my research, I found Dr. Sue Morter, who shared a philosophy called, The Bus Stop Talk. Paraphrasing, it happens when the soul travels to being human. Making "bus stops" along the way, we meet others and agree to help each other learn things. This idea blew my mind. The concept marinated. This perspective grew to show me the gift of forgiveness. Forgiveness doesn't mean he's off the hook for his actions; it means I'm not taking the poison of anger and hate and expecting him to feel the poisoning's effects. Forgiveness means I get to release the remaining festered pus that exploded on the Reiki table all those years ago. It means I get to move forward in life without the heaviness, sadness, guilt, and shame. Forgiveness allowed me to be free to be deeply and positively happy.

Forgiveness is an uneven road, and I'm a deeply-feeling human. Some days, I end up four-wheeling off-road, covered in mud. I'm grateful for having Reiki to provide the shower I need to wash off the mud and start again. Reiki deepened my personal sense of well-being and provided an avenue back to center. It opened my spiritual curiosity. Reiki showed me there are non-traditional ways to heal, and I'm deeply appreciative of these alternative methods that Reiki provided and led me to learn.

Today, as a Reiki Master with my own practice and a Master Teacher teaching others this beautiful technique. I love to share that healing doesn't have to be super hard; sometimes, a small shift in thinking or an experience can change everything. As a coach, I share this in many ways with my clients.

Are you ready for forgiveness? The following is a practice I and some of my clients have used. It can be emotional. It can be a little difficult. It can be transformational if you let it.

This excellent practice to work through and find forgiveness is writing a letter to that person who wronged you. This letter doesn't need to be sent, although it can be. My favorite thing to do is burn the letter after writing it. Take this practice another step. Write to yourself as if you were that person who wronged you. Again, they don't need to know. Tear the letter in tiny bits, burn it, flush it, and do what feels right with it for you.

I also recommend the bus stop questions: 1) What if he met me along the way and agreed to teach me something? 2) What if I agreed to teach him something?

I do loads of journaling and meditation on these questions; then I write those letters again.

Finding forgiveness gave me self-esteem and calmed my anxiety and negative emotions. It allowed me to decide how to let go. I am healthier and happier because of forgiveness.

A determined woman born to break barriers, **Lianne Hofer** proves that when fueled with purpose, women are unstoppable. She built her career and life one brick at a time, fighting fears, overcoming setbacks, and deciding failure is feedback. She inspires others as she personifies overcoming adversity. Through her courses and coaching, clients have experienced their own success with her as their champion. Lianne has been featured on podcasts and television, quoted in books, newspapers, and magazine articles, and enjoys sharing how others can change their lives when they are ready. Already an award-winning, international best-selling author, she is honored to participate in this beautiful and significant book. Lianne can be found at LianneHofer.com where she shares how to find the blueprint to design the happiness in your life.

CHAPTER 21

FROM BROKEN TO BEAUTY

HOW TO SHOW UP, HEAL, AND THRIVE

Martha Lazo-Muñoz

MY STORY

My early memories of my life are not very good. I experienced sexual abuse at a very young age, which would alter me for the rest of my life. I had some good experiences as a child, some of which come with positive memories, but they come with very mixed emotions as it has taken me years to heal and recover from the pain and trauma I experienced.

In 1956, a baby girl was born in El Paso, Texas. That baby girl was me. My mom, I have been told, was happy when this, her second child, arrived. My father, well, not so much as he was hoping for a boy. After two years, my parents decided life would be best in Los Angeles, California. After all, they thought, *there were family members already living in California and a job waiting*–a job for father. So off they went! With two little girls in tow, they packed up their belongings and set off to their new home in Los Angeles, California.

I was still quite young, and I hadn't a clue as to what was taking place, so it was difficult for me to recall specific details or specifics. But my life was going to change drastically, sooner rather than later.

I recall sitting out on our front porch with our uncles and aunties, my mom, and her favorite sister, Auntie Lucy. Years later, my Auntie Lucy would be my refuge, my safe place, and my comforter. She would give me some of the nurturing I needed. She demonstrated her love by reading books to me and combing my tangled hair. Auntie Lucy was and is ever so significant in my life! Every child needs an "Auntie Lucy."

I remember the cool breeze on my face with the sun setting, our father and his brother (my uncle) playing guitars, my father playing his harmonica, and the singing. Mostly these songs were Spanish love ballads, as I recall, with some jazzy sounds. My uncle, Dad's brother, Leo, had quite a good voice. He would take the lead, and Father would follow thereafter. These were some of the good fond memories I recall during our summers.

I can still see my mother in my mind's eye. She was so beautiful, with her long wavy hair, slender body frame, and her smile when things were good between her and my father. My father, though, was known in the family for his "disappearing act." Dad would suddenly leave for a few days and sometimes even weeks. I remember those days more starkly because I could hear my mother crying in the evening. As a child, I didn't understand why she cried so much when Dad was gone. Mother appeared to work harder at home when he went away, with laundry, dishes, cooking, and taking care of us children. Eventually, Mother gave birth to her third child, another baby girl.

As a child, one doesn't know what is going on with one's parents. We're so trusting and believe grownups know what to do. However, it seemed my mother became more distant at times, almost as if in a fog. I can see myself pulling on her apron, pleading, "Mom," but she didn't respond. As I understand it now, she was depressed. It was such a sad time for me; this was the beginning of the many times I called out to Mother, and she was not available mentally, emotionally, or physically. I longed for my mother to hold me, hug me, and tell me everything would be alright, but she seldom did; I don't think she could, as I believe she, too, longed for her mother's love. Like my grandmother and those who came before her, my mother called on her faith in her God to sustain her and took us to a Catholic church to find our salvation. There were pros and cons to churchgoing, but it taught us about faith in a higher power: about God, Jesus Christ.

I did not have the opportunity to meet my grandmother since she died long before I was born. After my grandmother gave birth to my youngest uncle, she had ongoing complications from the birthing. My mother would share stories about her mom: how good of a cook my grandmother was and how well she cared for her home. Perhaps my mother's focus on those parts of being a wife and mother, along with her faith in God, stemmed from my grandmother's focus on these things.

Grandmother had seven children. My grandfather, I was told, was a hard worker. My grandparents had a ranch or farm and raised chickens, goats, and pigs. They sold eggs and had a little mini-store in New Mexico, a little town called Fierro. It was called "Francisco Nava store," named after my grandfather's father. Perhaps this is what catalyzed my entrepreneurial spirit!

The spirit of my mother and grandmother stayed with me, formed, and bolstered me. I would need their strength in the years to come. The cleaning of the home and the focus on remaining busy resonates with me; my mother was keeping herself busy to distract herself from thinking about where my father was or when he would be coming home. Unfortunately, there were no skills in effective communication nor an understanding of the family's dysfunction. My family members simply did not know there was a better way of life!

Years past. I was about four or five years of age the first time I was sexually abused. We had a very nice, friendly neighbor: Larry. He was married, but I don't recall his wife's name. All I can remember is that this Larry man would come over and talk to my father quite a bit when Dad was home. Larry and his wife brought us girls treats, cookies, candies, and coloring books. My family often could not afford these things, so we appreciated this a lot (even though it did not register to me that we were "poor" or what that meant).

How wonderful to be getting these gifts, we all thought. Unbeknownst to any of us, including me, I was being groomed. "Grooming" is a word to describe when a predator is gaining a child's trust–and the parent's as well. Predators give you gifts and kind words; they go out of their way to show you and the parents how much they care, but they are like a "wolf in sheep's clothing." Other terms found in Christian teachings that describe this are "seducing or lustful spirits."

As I walked past our neighbor's house, Larry would be outside watering his lawn, waiting for me. I can still hear his voice saying, "Come inside; I want to show you something." I can still feel his hand grabbing me and pulling me inside his house or garage, where he could lock the door. While I endured the abuse, I thought, *this is not right,* and the candy he gave me just after confused me further. Along with that bag of candy were his words, "Don't tell anyone, not your mother or your father," which frightened me. *Why not?! What would happen?* I often sobbed afterward and could not understand how my mother could not read my face and know something was wrong. I became withdrawn and quiet and didn't care to bathe or comb my hair. I had long curly hair like my mother. But she didn't even notice something was wrong. Or Maybe she did and was too afraid to ask or "really know."

After years of abuse in Los Angeles, California, we finally moved and left that house. I was happy! I thought I was safe. But not so fast! It seemed everywhere we moved, there was someone else abusing me. Now, it was not just strangers but distant male family members. I felt like I had become someone else; to protect myself and my mind, I hid who I really was. That sweet innocent child had so much anger, so much rage. I became a bully! By middle school, in my early teens, I was rough and tough. I became a "tomboy," a tough girl so no one could ever hurt me again! Or so I thought. I played every sport I could get into. I became quite the athlete. I enjoyed track and field sports and baseball with the neighborhood kids, mostly boys, since I was so determined to hurt boys and men.

I had so much hurt and pain inside me, and I always wanted and longed for an adult to notice and comfort me, but no one did. There was no one to save me, no one to rescue me. I had only one person from whom I could receive unconditional love—my Auntie Lucy. Although I believe she was also limited in her skills and knowledge of what to do, she was quite comforting. I was a child living with pain and trauma.

But that would change. I would change all that. I would find my way.

THE PRACTICE

Deep within my core, I sensed something was wrong. I desired and found answers. At the age of 23 or thereabouts, I began my healing journey. I see my healing as an act of God. I believe my faith saved me from myself. These years later, I would learn from those teachings of the church long ago. My faith sustained me.

My yearning to get and obtain knowledge and wisdom propelled me forward. I was hungry for education and wanted answers. I knew what happened to me was not normal behavior or living.

I signed up for college classes. My counselor asked, "What will be your major?" I had no clue! I just wanted to learn! As one longs for, seeks, and hungers for knowledge and wisdom, God places the right people on the path and manifests what is needed. My counselor suggested a class called Life Learning. *What was this,* I thought, but it turned out it was not only a good thing, it was also the right thing, along with a major in marketing and some focus on math and English toward an associate degree.

When I entered college, I was already married with two small children. I married their father at the age of sixteen. I was a teenager when I married since I became pregnant and the only option in my family was to marry. Due to all my issues, this marriage did not last, though we remained good friends. That's another story!

At any rate, back to school it was for me. I was beginning to believe in myself, and I was so happy to do something so great just for me! I felt empowered and liberated for once in my life. My teachers, college classes, and courses also helped me heal.

One of my professors happened to be a therapist! She was the coolest, hippy-looking teacher! I liked her as she reminded me of me during my high school days! One day after class, she called me over to her desk, asked if we could chat, and I said, "Sure." After all, she was cool.

She began asking me about my life, which I found interesting. *Why is she asking me these questions?* I thought. But I felt so safe with her that I began to tell her my story. To this day, we remain close friends. I am so thankful to God for placing her in my life and on my journey! I began to see her regularly on a professional basis. This is where she taught me about dysfunctional families, sexually abused children, behaviors, traumas and triggers, and so much more. I was like a sponge, I longed for more information, wisdom, and knowledge. I would attend training, seminars, classes – anything I could find. This teacher would turn out to be the tip of the iceberg regarding my healing for my family and me. I used these means and my faith to continue my healing journey.

This was my course to healing. I believe that if you have a longing, a desire within you to want to be better, God is there for you too! I am just one human being on this planet here to help serve and guide you toward your healing! There is something better for you too!

Today, I am the CEO/Founder of Women with Hope Ministry. Today, I teach women who have experienced Domestic Violence. They come to me from all backgrounds: healthcare professionals, stay-at-home moms, college and high school students, and those within the church. I teach them how to identify triggers associated with traumas, how to know what the red flags are in toxic relationships, what narcissistic behaviors are, and how to identify emotional, mental, and physical abuse. The level of one's education, background, and socioeconomic status doesn't matter–rich or poor, well-educated or not, white or blue or domestic worker, domestic violence holds no boundaries.

Wisdom from above is what we all need! Manifestations happen when you pray, look for, and position yourself to receive all the goodness this universe has to offer! God's love is here for us all.

Martha Lazo-Munoz is the CEO and Founder of Women with Hope Ministry. She teaches those who have experienced domestic violence, from healthcare professionals to stay-at-home moms, college students, high school students, and within churches. She teaches you how to identify triggers associated with traumas, how to know what the red flags in a toxic relationship are, and also about narcissistic behaviors, and how to identify emotional, mental, and physical abuse. Martha wants you to know that it matters not the level of one's education, background, rich or poor—domestic violence holds no boundaries. Wisdom from above is what we all need! Manifestations happen when you pray, look for, and position yourself to receive all the goodness this universe has to offer! God's love is here for all of us.

Connect with Martha:

https://www.womanslegacy.org

https://linktr.ee/womanslegacy

https://www.facebook.com/womenslegacyofhope/

WhatsApp: 619-207-7703

CHAPTER 22

EMBRACING THE SELVES

LEARNING TO GROW FROM TRAUMA

Sylvie Manti, Diploma Hum.Psych, Bsc(hons), MPhil.

MY STORY

When I was six years old, my world changed direction for the first time. This was when the first of my selves emerged in response to what I endured.

Everything I knew or thought I knew, which was sugar-coated and filled with laughter, became covered in a thick greasy silence. I couldn't speak for fear of being found out, being blamed, being misunderstood, or the worst thing, being accused of lying.

Cypriot family life in the 1970s and 1980s was a homage to patriarchy and filled with rights and wrongs always tied to the honor code system—a system based on the virtue and virginity of the female as a currency for family honor, standing, and the path to a respected and lauded marriage where I'd pass from my father's protection to my husband's.

My honor was gone; I knew that. Even at six years old, I knew it. After my first self emerged, other parts of me emerged over time, branching out. This was a coping mechanism, a mode of survival that gave me a semblance of control. I learned ways of being that shielded and protected me, and sometimes even made me feel empowered and in control.

I never gave different names to the branches of my *self*, although I've spoken and shared with others who have.

Since my sixth year, I've walked into, traveled through, and been dragged and duped to by many other traumas. Some are just as painful as the first. Decades later, now in my fifties, faced with stage IV breast cancer with metastasis to the brain, liver, and bones, I know my time is limited. Yet, through this latest and probably last trauma (which I have come to call a challenge), I've been afforded the opportunity to look back and evaluate my life and learnings. Sharing this learning here, I hope that even if you didn't branch out into selves like I did, but found your own ways of coping, surviving, and hopefully thriving, you can add this perspective and soar even higher.

The first *self* I knew about came on top of the trauma, hand in hand, and was hence the hardest to embrace, yet with healing, became my wisest *self*.

My first *self* was a silent one. I was wracked with the guilt of the duplicity of allowing my family to believe their honor was intact, and throttled by the fear that I might upset the Almighty by speaking out. I was encouraged to believe God was all-seeing and all-knowing and would punish my family if I spoke out. The six-year-old child changed from an incessantly chatty attention-grabbing prima donna to a quiet, silent, and observant shadow, hiding under long tablecloths and always sitting low in the back of the room to be noticed as little as possible. Embracing the silent one, I learned the virtue of observation, the safety in assessing a situation before stepping in, and the advantage of giving space to others to express and define themselves and their intentions before I stepped in, so I could gauge them better and hence feel safer. This afforded me a sense of clarity and control in tense, unfamiliar or threatening situations. As a parent, a peacebuilder, and a therapist, this *self* has served me well. The silent, watchful me can often feel childlike and wide-eyed in my mind, whereas outwardly, she absorbs like a sponge.

Quickly, off the back of this *self*, came the male *self*, a self based on the belief that if I was one of the privileged patriarchal class, I'd be dominant and in control and therefore never hurt. This branch of me busied itself with emulating and assimilating male attitudes and behaviors. I learned to strut, to walk into a room as if entitled, and to affect self-important behaviors and leadership traits which I'd practice in the safety of my friend group. I wanted so much to be male, thinking this would save me from trauma.

As I faced the world, I discovered, disturbingly, that everyone I know has trauma, male or female. When I became an adult and was involved in LGBTQIA+ work, I realized it was all other gender orientations too. This branch of me came into its own when working as a peacebuilder. Working in an invariably male environment filled with smoldering sparks of possible conflict at every turn, this *self* sat next to my silent *self* and often gave me advantageous insight into male-dominant conflict situations, helping me feel a semblance of control. My body posture, level of eye contact, and the scenes I watched play out in male family feuds, where my father, uncles, and cousins strutted and postured, were channeled through this part of me. Men responded by feeling as if I understood them and as if they could confide in me like I was one of them. Although this branch of myself rarely makes itself felt now, as a young woman making her way in the world, I found myself drawing frequently on this part of myself as a kind of protective shield, helping to embolden me and steady my fear of being dominated and hurt again.

Sometime in my pre-teen years, I continued to hide under tables, but now with books. I became an avid reader, reading everything from children's books to books well above my pay grade, including ill-fated love stories and horror, via the classics. I discovered that if I held a book open and stared at it, I was largely left alone. This granted me precious alone time; no one bothered me, therefore, they couldn't hurt me.

It also meant I could escape from the crushing and heavy reality of holding the secret that I was living my life in the solitary squalor of the sin of breaking the family honor by having somehow lost the only thing I was responsible for—the family honor. I traveled far and wide through books and learned I wasn't alone.

The most important lesson I learned from all the fiction and fantasy I consumed was I could have a happy ending if I chose to. This is my go-to when I'm in doubt or when yet another challenge threatens to derail me.

Sometimes, especially now faced with stage IV brain metastases, I feel like I'm falling into a dark and deep hole, as I did when I was a child. It is a damp, lonely, and cold place where seemingly all I can do is curl up and wait for the end. This can, on the surface, feel like a just punishment for someone who took her eye off the ball and crashed the family honor.

In these times, I draw on my imaginative branch, searching for different endings and hoped-for beginnings. The process of fleshing out, building on, and coloring in a path for myself has always been a personal journey. I'm filled with empowered, strong, hopeful, and joyous possibilities. This part of me reigns strong whenever I notice the cold sweat on my neck, the shallow, painful breathing of shock, and the instinctual feelings of fear that rise up from my stomach and knock on the door of my emotions.

Having been tormented with black thoughts and rooms in my mind and a feeling of always being lost, the *self* that found an anchor emerged. It was fleeting, never staying more than a moment longer than needed to anchor me, to provide me a beacon in the darkness. All this *self* would do is ask for a number from someone trusted and safe. Most times, any number would do, sometimes a number between, say, 50 and 200. I focus on that number, the spelling, sound and shape of it, the mini or magnitude of it. It becomes a point of focus, an anchor in the dark, to save me from the feeling of drifting uncontrollably. When I was a child, I asked my parents, friends, or my cousins for a number. This was harmless, incomprehensible to them and yet soul-saving for me. It was a survival mechanism that went unnoticed. During my university years, when sexual freedom was considered part of the process, asking my roommate or a trusted boyfriend for a number would steady me in the sea of drunken parties where people made out happily and openly, and I silently hunkered in the corner, bewildered. When the oncologist explained that metastasis to the brain meant possibly a quicker death, within a few months at most if the chemo drugs could not hold it, I turned to my partner and asked for a number, "Any number." I needed to hold on to something to not lose myself in the enormity of it all. This is a *self* I rely on when I need to survive so I can give myself time to work out how to thrive.

Soon after, in my late teens or early twenties, I discovered the intellectual *self.* Having marveled at people talking in public and having something to say and being listened to, my silent *self* watched, observed, and understood the power this afforded them. I wanted that too. This became my survival mode default. Claiming essay deadlines and thesis rewrites, I stepped away from the frightened silent child who stared with open eyes at those around her and disguised my*self* as an authority on feminism, rights, politics, or philosophy—anything that kept the subject matter far and safely away from me. This *self* took me through college, university, and career placements.

Absorbing every piece of knowledge that came my way, I developed as a thriver absorbing her surroundings.

Being watchful, silent, observant, and intellectual—these selves lent themselves effortlessly to a parent who stood beside her children with a gentle hand, engaged with communities posturing on the brink between peace and war, and who sat beside the client seeking therapeutic insight backed with theory. I learned to thrive and not just to survive. I learned trauma and challenges would come my way, and that sometimes I can't foresee them or sidestep past them, yet I have the skills, the *selves,* to work out how to keep moving and thriving. Self-reflection and small wins encourage me to come back to myself, draw on myself, believe in myself, and trust I can and will find a way.

With my *selves* I don't feel alone, and, most importantly, I don't feel vulnerable. More recently, they are seamless and less distinct than when I was younger, a pleasant and social merging where I can explore my process and next steps.

THE PRACTICE

I've learned many things, and I hope they might help you. In my life and work, I've learned that to heal and grow, you need a focus on finding power and acceptance from within, and using experience (whatever experience teaches us) as a learning tool for growth and empowerment. Using this orientation, I discovered we could achieve individual and group potential, action planning, and effect positive change, whoever we are.

What taught me the most was a gained ability to focus on and notice the transition from trauma to surviving and then thriving. I was so busy believing I was surviving that when I started to thrive, it went unnoticed for a time. It's important to stay cognizant of what's happening to you.

Although at times my journey seemed as though it was invisible and seamless, it was a journey and one that was deliberate, often tumultuous, and filled with disappointments and despair, as well as with wins and understanding.

I've learned that with the wins come strength and acceptance. I've learned to embrace and love these *selves* of mine. I was guided by a light in the dark from Carl Rogers, who wisely pointed out "that when I accept my*self* as I am, then I change." (1988). He called it a 'curious paradox.' It was the beginning of understanding that who I was before each trauma, as with each joy, and who I am after each trauma, as with each joy, is who I am. With this came peace.

Sylvie completed her studies in the UK in counseling psychotherapy, focusing on women's rights and using experience as a learning tool for change. With almost 30 years of experience in facilitation, from one-to-one work to facilitation work with civil society, conflicted communities, and groups, Sylvie has a proven track record in successful facilitation. She strives to bring partner groups together in a positive working environment even when there is a pre-existing conflict. With a keen interest in working on human rights issues and growth, Sylvie has concentrated on women's issues, youth, and LGBTQIA+ rights. However, in the last decade, some of her work has included being part of a core team based in Cyprus, working on larger conflicts such as the Cyprus problem, bringing together Israeli and Palestinian participants to find common-ground facilitation work in the Arab region, advocating for the protection from physical and sexual abuse of young people with learning difficulties, and lastly working with the medical community advocating for patient rights in terms of treatment plans and decision-making. Her work focuses on power from within, using experience as learning for growth and empowerment while guiding towards individual and group potential, action planning, and effecting positive change.

CHAPTER 23

FROM ABUSED, TRAUMATIZED, IMMIGRANT CHILD TO POWERFUL MAN, COMMUNITY LEADER, AND ENTREPRENEUR

TAKING A BROKEN CHILDHOOD AND BUILDING A LIFE FULFILLED

Akerei Maresala-Thomson

MY STORY

Talofa. Akerei Maresala-Thomson is my full name. I'm originally from Samoa. New Zealand is my adopted country. I'm a child sexual abuse survivor, suicide survivor, and former youth gang member who turned his life around, becoming a Senior Sergeant, community leader, and entrepreneur. This is my story, but not only my story. It's the story of many of my people.

I come from a long line of strong Polynesian chiefs. We are, as a people, the greatest navigators in history. To be the greatest navigators in over 3,000 years, we had to be masters of science, technology, engineering, and math. So, please know that some of the STEM subjects that people try to shove down the throats of my people, saying that these are new things from the Western world that will save our people, we've been using for many years.

But despite being a warrior people and the greatest navigators in history, we're also not exempt from some challenges others are confronting, including suicide. As a people, we have one of the highest suicide rates in the Organization for Economic Cooperation and Development (OECD), where 37 democracies develop policy standards to promote sustainable economic growth.

We, as a people, try to deal with our problems through traditional and non-traditional ways. The Haka, for example, is a form of expression. Some call it a dance. That's not quite right; it's a performance to try and put fear in your enemies. It's also used as a traditional cultural tool to challenge the status quo, including some of the social issues prevalent in my community.

I wanted to help. I'm not a doctor or clinician; I suppose if I needed a title, the best label would be "entrepreneur." I'm an entrepreneur, having spent many years trying to navigate life as a young son—one boy who moved to New Zealand with his family at a very young age to a community that was supposed to be the land of opportunity.

There are generally three key life pillars that Polynesians believe provide support, which is critical to our identity:

1. We are strong people of culture.

2. We are a people of faith and spiritual focus.

3. Family is a protective factor.

If any of these pillars are broken, there's a good chance that whatever anyone is doing or trying to do when attempting to mentor and support a Polynesian kid, they're going to have some problems unless they address some of those key pillars.

So, imagine being a four-year-old in Samoa where you grow up with those key values, those protective factors underscored, where you go to church every day, and the person on the pulpit preaches about love, empathy, compassion, and God. Imagine after they do that, that later that day, they come into your room and start doing what they want to do with you.

And then you move to another country where all you're focused on is trying to learn this language called English. And the man on the pulpit (my uncle) moves into your three-bedroom state house in South Auckland. We were one of the first of our family to move to that South Auckland state house, so it became the hub for every other relative to move there.

A lot of dynamics shifted when we moved to New Zealand. In Samoa, I saw Mum and Dad every day. We went to the sea to collect water and food and to the plantation and gathered crops. We cooked, cleaned, and did everything together. Now, in this foreign "land of milk and honey," we didn't see Mum and Dad until Sundays–the one day off for these spiritual people.

As a headquarters space for other Samoans moving over, it wasn't uncommon to have 30 people living under one roof with me and my six siblings. We didn't know whether they were relatives, neighbors, or neighbors' neighbors. These people started looking after us. One of them was the same uncle that did that stuff to me.

Nobody told me what sex was or what was right or wrong in that regard. In school, other kids were talking about it. It became apparent that it wasn't just me going through this in isolation in my own home. By the age of seven, with all that going on in New Zealand, I told my parents (one of my key strong pillars, right?). "I think what so-and-so is doing to me is wrong." They beat me up, and I had to eat porridge for the next couple of weeks because "how dare I talk about the uncle like that—without my uncle, we wouldn't have had the finances to get to New Zealand!" We were blessed. Right? Man of the cloth.

Through those pillars, I tried to seek refuge and support, but each time I reached out, I got none. I joined a gang because my uncles were in a gang, the Respect Samoan Bloods. My first suicide attempt was at age nine, followed by an attempt at 12. And it was generally my sisters who were the ones who helped me out of it.

My situation wasn't unique. It was common among people like me and other Polynesians in New Zealand. There were a lot of people telling these stories; there were a lot of Hakas going on across New Zealand.

We're a warrior people, but we're dying in unnatural numbers. In 2016, Polynesian young boys surpassed the suicide rate of the boys belonging to the indigenous people of New Zealand, the Māori, who've been treated so badly. In 2016, our women died faster than Māori women resulting from interpersonal violence.

I became a very violent young man. I was kicked out of four high schools. I took a machete to school and tried to kill my teacher. I hardly went home and just did what I wanted. Because of my failures at school, my family sent me back to Samoa.

But my people were the best navigators in history because the Polynesian people never traveled alone. They always traveled in pairs, at a minimum. I use this as an analogy to highlight the critical role of helpers in the lives of not only my people but the lives of the individuals, families, and the people.

When I returned to New Zealand, a local good police officer oversaw my case. He said, "You're a big guy. You've got a lot of issues and anger, but you can use your anger and frustrations on the rugby field, and people might pay you to hurt people on the field, professionally." And that sounded really good to me. So, when I was 20, I had the opportunity to play professional rugby in France, Wales, England, Ireland, and Northern Ireland.

Then I returned home, and I joined the police force.

I thought this was the last job I wanted to do; I hated the police. But I believed I had value—I could help them provide empathy and compassion so they could better work with my community. There was also value for me to learn and be a role model by taking ideas back to my church, community, and my family. I began protecting the toughest suburbs in New Zealand, the very mean streets on which I used to cause trouble. I spent a lot of time picking up truants and returning them to school. At six-foot-two inches and 135 kilograms (297 pounds), I was a pretty imposing force and was able to make an impression in and help protect my community. If we could stop or minimize the offending, then we could stop or minimize the number of victims of crime.

I noticed the high numbers of truants were the same as the high numbers of burglaries and petty thefts. We went out and picked up every truant and returned them to school. Those two weeks corresponded with our lowest-ever burglaries.

I also helped them find jobs. One gang member was withdrawing money from an ATM when a police car drove by. For the first time, he wasn't worried because he was using his own card and withdrawing his own money, which he'd earned working.

We were dealing with three high-profile murders at one point, which left the public on edge. After another six homicides, the government had a knee-jerk reaction and set up Youth Action Teams. They told us to go out and do what New Zealand had been doing since the 1860s since the establishment of the police force: go out and arrest everybody and throw them in jail.

I challenged them. There's a Samoan proverb that says, *E fofo e le alamea le alamea*. Alamea is a poisonous crownfish. Ancient Samoan fishermen say if you stand on the thorns of a crown fish, they inject you with poison. To pull out the poison, you turn the crown fish on its back, and you place its spongy-like feet on the wound of the area. The analogy is: "solutions for issues in the community can be found in that community."

We asked our bosses, "Instead of just getting outsiders to come in and try and fix the problems in this community, why don't we go and ask the families of the perpetrators and victims what the solution looks like to them?" After 12 years of attending suicides and homicides across New Zealand, I've never attended one homicide or suicide that ever happened in Parliament or the council chambers where all the policies and legislations were being signed off. They all happened in my home, backyard, or my community.

One of the news stations reported about me, recognizing I had a unique perspective. They told about how I used to be a gang member and how I hated the police, but then became a part of the Youth Action Team, helping to get gang members off the streets. In the interview, I said: "When seven friends first met each other, we were all involved in gangs: one committed suicide, one died of a drug overdose, one died of leukemia, and one died as a teen drunk driving. Three of us are alive, but one bloke was jailed two years ago for armed robbery, and one has a pending assault case." I'm the lucky one. As my friends dropped off, one by one, I made changes for the better–for me and others. At that point, I was 30 and alive and not in jail. I could hardly have been any more on the right side of the law. I'm the only one out of the seven friends that made it!

Accountability—we're a warrior people. We're masters of science, technology, engineering, and math; we're entrepreneurs by trade. We can come up with meaningful and sustainable solutions for our community. When one of the kids I worked with said, "We only get help from these services after we get in trouble," I knew it was an important point. Eighty percent of referrals in New Zealand come via the hospitals, police, and courts after someone has either committed suicide, a crime, or become a victim.

I knew how hard it was for my family and me when we moved from Samoa to New Zealand in the 1980s. I wanted to help. That was what led me to be an entrepreneur and what led to our MYRIVR solution–an app my partners and I identified that gives people a way of directly contacting more than 7,000 organizations and 20,000 professionals who can help with providing all types of answers for people they actually want and need. MYRIVR is designed to help people talk. I didn't do it alone, and it wasn't and isn't mine. Solutions come via the kids and others, and they are good ones. I'm a navigator. I go find people to make those things happen.

I'm passionate about this. I know we're helping our people. Polynesians coming to New Zealand can now get the information and the answers they need to be comfortable and confident arriving in New Zealand. We help them with tasks from understanding how to get a driver's license to getting a family doctor. These simple and more complex pieces of information are helping so many people. We've expanded to other states across Australia and New Zealand. We've now won several awards.

And then: Curveball! Imagine doing all that, winning awards, and then finding out your father has been imprisoned for rape. Before that, I talked with my father about my situation, how so many bad things happened to me when I was a kid, and how it wasn't unique to me. I thought he was there for me. Then, with all that I'd done to correct the problems, I found out that my father had a problem and was a perpetrator himself. This is a very recent development.

Last year, during my niece's 21st birthday, he raped a young girl. And some people may even be thinking: *shit, man, this guy has won awards and is speaking internationally and doing all these cool things, but he can't even solve problems in his own backyard.* I have a very different "take" on this. Had I not attended things like the IVAT Summit in 2017, I wouldn't have been surrounded by other worldviews and ways of doing things or been able to apply them. And now I can.

One of the things I could do was have a sit-down meeting with my siblings because we'd never discussed having been sexually abused by my dad's family. One by one, every one of my siblings disclosed their own abuse.

One of them was my young sister. I couldn't figure out why my sister was sent to live with other relatives in Australia. I was on my own journey of discovery, trying to figure out what the fuck happened to me. At the same time, every other family member was on their own journey, trying to figure out what the fuck happened to them.

My sister was molested by my dad at the age of 15. Four years ago, he did the same thing to her daughter, his *moko* [grandchild], and my other sister's daughter. As a family, we found the courage and resilience to break boundaries and barriers to all the secrets and silence. We decided, *fuck that; it's gone on for too long.* We went with this young lady to make her complaint so that this guy, my father, could be held accountable.

That opened up a lot of cans of worms. We had to go and share that information with Dad's sisters. If he had done this for this long and was now in his 70s, it was likely it had happened before. Remember, there were 30 people living under our roof at any given time.

To date, we know there are at least ten other victims.

In addition, a month after my dad went to prison, a lot of other shit happened.

My brother went to prison last month: Gang shootings in South Auckland. The day after he went to prison, his room got shot out by the opposing gang.

This is heavy stuff, I know. I'm writing this because I know those reading this want change and want to help others and that a lot of you trying to help people are going through some similar crazy shit. But we can make a difference—together.

I come from a long line of awesome warriors and entrepreneurs. I know now that I'm one of them. Join me.

THE PRACTICE

We must recognize that we cannot handle all this alone. We have to reach out. We must build on what we and others have and work together. We can help each other and our communities by doing so. Everybody has a role to play in a person's life. This is a simple message that is not so easy to accomplish.

This point took root for me, in part, when I started doing some work with my colleague and friend, the lead author of this book, Pamela J. Pine, from Stop the Silence®. I realized my story wasn't unique and that many people were telling similar stories.

I started to call more on my own background and community, and so can you. Use the good parts of your culture to guide you; allow the spirit to move you; call on trusted family members, your friendships, and your collegial relationships to support you. But think of what works and what doesn't for you—have faith in that voice inside you that tells you what is right and working and what is not.

I want to end with something I'm very proud of to illustrate these points. Most recently, I have focused on the economics of our people. We come from a warrior people, but we often see them, especially during COVID, in Food Bank queues, relying on government handouts and aid. In response, I now help indigenous communities set up their own self-sustaining businesses. The Pasifika Digital Knowledge Bank is a facility designed to be an incubator of Māori and Pacifica-led solutions, helping indigenous populations grow their entrepreneurial ideas and address their well-being, so they're no longer held back. It's now up and running in a 614-square-meter space! I hope that this focus will be multi-generational. When I and others I work with now are no longer here, we want somebody else to come and take over. I want to see the chain continue.

This work is teaching my people to be both connected to themselves and others while being self-sufficient and self-reliant. Good practices for us all.

Akerei Maresala-Thomson, MBA

Akerei (Rei) Maresla-Thomson is a child sexual abuse survivor, suicide survivor, and former youth gang member who turned his life around, becoming a Senior Sergeant, community leader, and entrepreneur. He is a social architect and Co-Founder of the award-winning free community MYRIVR app developed and presented by Trust MYRIVR. It is the largest in app directory in New Zealand, with a goal to become the largest enabler of community services in the world. He is also the founder and CEO of the Pasifika Digital Knowledge Bank, a facility designed to be an incubator of Māori and Pacifica-led solutions, helping indigenous populations grow their entrepreneurial ideas and address their well-being. Previously, he was the former General Manager of the Village Collective, an innovative Pacific NGO based in Auckland that delivers sexual health prevention programs across New Zealand. He served for 12 years in the New Zealand Police Service as a ranking Senior Sergeant where he managed the Pacific, Ethnic, and Asian portfolios for Counties Manukau District, and he coordinated the Police National Radio Language Program. Akerei also held a strategic international position for nearly ten years as a technical advisor training local police of small island nations across the South Pacific region and advocating on pre-migration issues. He is passionate about preventing domestic violence and innovations for positive social outcomes. He is New Zealand's 86th White Ribbon Ambassador. Trust MYRIVR is a formal partner of Stop the Silence® in the U.S. (https://ivatcenters.org/stop-the-silence). The partners are working to bring comprehensive CSA prevention and mitigation programs to countries across the world that includes the MYRIVR App.

Connect with Rei through:

akerei@myrivr.co.nz

www.myrivr.co.nz

CONCLUSION

WHAT CAN WE DO TOGETHER TO STOP CSA?

Through the chapters of this book, I hope you can feel both the pain and the healing that is possible and related by our authors.

I'd like to conclude this book with a bit of reiteration and a call to action:

> "Every year, millions of girls and boys around the world face sexual abuse and exploitation. Sexual violence occurs everywhere–in every country and across all segments of society. A child may be subjected to sexual abuse or exploitation at home, at school, or in their community. The widespread use of digital technologies can also put children at risk. Most often, abuse occurs at the hands of someone a child knows and trusts. At least 120 million girls under the age of 20– about 1 in 10–have been forced to engage in sex or perform other sexual acts, although the actual figure is likely much higher. Roughly 90 percent of adolescent girls who report forced sex say that their first perpetrator was someone they knew, usually a boyfriend or a husband. But many victims of sexual violence, including millions of boys, never tell anyone." (UNICEF, https://www.unicef.org/protection/sexual-violence-against-children, retrieved November 9, 2022)

CSA results in a host of poor outcomes for children, the adults they become, and society at large. CSA severely affects our behavior, neurology, a broad spectrum of mental and physical health outcomes, life expectancy, and the monetary cost to nations.

This is just blatantly and obviously unacceptable. Without proper intervention, the consequences of CSA often last through adulthood (the average age at which survivors in the U.S. tell anyone, if they tell anyone, is 52), affecting us all.

Please make it a priority to learn more about CSA and ACEs: who they affect, how it happens, and ways that you can get involved–and then please do, on whatever level you can. Let's, together, protect the children, support survivors, and bring change to society.

Pamela J. Pine, Ph.D., MPH

Director, Stop the Silence® – A Department of the Institute on Violence, Abuse and Trauma, https://www.ivatcenters.org/stop-the-silence

April 2023

ACKNOWLEDGEMENTS – WITH GRATITUDE

Many moons ago, I wrote in my high school yearbook something like: "I want to thank those who made these years enjoyable and tolerable – and, in a strange way, to those who did the opposite."

There are probably thousands of people who should be acknowledged who have brought us to this place in various ways. In the "enjoyable and tolerable" category, in addition to people like Sandi Capuano Morrison, CEO, IVAT, who is just exemplary as a leader in every way (she listens, she asks, she believes in, she supports, she tells you what she thinks, she is knowledgeable, thoughtful, flexible, kind, caring – I could go on), there are so many supporters and colleagues who have made a difference in the work and in my life (please forgive me if I have left out anyone). These include all the authors in this book as well as Amy Pine, and colleagues like Robert Geffner, Edward Schline, Victor Vieth, Vincent Felitti, Eileen King, Ernestine Briggs-King, Akerei Maresala-Thomson and Elia Chan of Trust MYRIVR, Joann Stevelos, Lindsay Thomason of The Nanny League, Craig Hansen of UARD, Ernestine Briggs-King, Lisa Conradi, Anthony Mannarino, Hilary Hodgdon, Robin Gurwitch, Stacie LeBlanc, Pearl Berman, Jacob Wilkins (my extraordinary first hire!), of course, Laura Di Franco, and so many more.

Then there are those who, very early on, supported and bolstered Stop the Silence® administratively, programmatically, and/or politically, and made it possible to move forward, like now-Congressman (!) Glenn Ivey, Senator Barbara Mikulski, Joan Pitkin, Pat Troy, Jeff Jordan, Sandra Rivera, Carmen Rodriguez, LaQuisha Hall, Emily Samuelson, Nicholas Panebianco, Nora Sjoblom Sanchez, Sharon Simone, Stuart Adam, and Michele Booth Cole (Safeshores-the DC Advocacy Center).

There are truly so many more to thank from government organizations, foundations, and corporate entities who have helped us along the way with funding or in-kind generosity. Thank you.

And also, to those who have done the opposite at times of making my work and life tolerable, from whom I also learned very important lessons: well, they know who they are; my hope is that they have learned important lessons, as well.

ABOUT THE AUTHOR

Pamela J. Pine, Ph.D., MPH, is an international public health/development professional, professor, and the Founder and Former CEO of Stop the Silence®: Stop Child Sexual Abuse, Inc. (Stop the Silence®), which, as of January 1, 2021, became Stop the Silence® - A Department of the Institute on Violence, Abuse and Trauma (IVAT) (https://ivatcenters.org/stop-the-silence). Pamela began working on child sexual abuse (CSA), other adverse childhood experiences (ACEs), and related issues of interpersonal violence and trauma in the year 2000. The focus of the Stop the Silence® Department is to prevent, expose, and stop CSA, ACEs, and related forms of interpersonal violence and trauma and help survivors heal worldwide. The Department carries out the work on CSA and other ACEs and trauma in close collaboration with government, non-profit, for-profit, and community-based groups through evidence-based, creative, and impactful programs that are carried out locally, nationally, and internationally. Pamela developed and has tested a workable CSA/ACE prevention/mitigation model adaptable for use in any country in the world and led by local presence.

Pamela's current and past work has focused on designing, developing, managing, implementing, and providing technical assistance to a wide range of health and related programs (e.g., awareness-raising/advocacy, training, community outreach, and education, community mobilization, media outreach, social marketing, policy development) concentrated on enhancing the lives of the poor and otherwise underserved groups for over 30 years. She has worked and/or presented on numerous specific areas (e.g., reproductive health, HIV/AIDS, leprosy, T.B., immunization, nutrition, maternal/child health, CSA and other interpersonal violence, microenterprise) throughout the world (e.g., Albania, Botswana, Congo (DRC), Cyprus, Ecuador, Egypt, the E.U., U.K., Haiti, Hungary, India, Italy, Jordan, New Zealand, Philippines, Poland, Qatar, South Africa, Switzerland, Tunisia, Turkey, United Kingdom, United States, Yemen, Zambia). She is considered an expert in CSA and trauma prevention and mitigation, including the at-risk nature of orphans and vulnerable children (OVC), sex trafficking, and related issues. She is called upon by TV, radio, and magazines to provide expert input on a regular basis. She speaks Arabic and French.

Pamela currently is the Director of Stop the Silence® - A Department of IVAT, where her primary current projects have to do with advocacy (e.g., through this book, through a traveling art exhibit gifted to Stop the Silence® by Jan Goff-Lafontaine, https://janlafontaine.com), education (an accredited online degree program to help put the world on the same page), and training (of many audiences). She also speaks internationally on CSA and related issues, provides assistance to national/international health/development programs and projects, and teaches public health at the university Masters' and Baccalaureate levels. She was honored in 2017 with a Lifetime Achievement Award in Advocacy from IVAT.

Pamela is on the Board of the National Partnership to End Interpersonal Violence (NPEIV); on the Advisory Committee of the Institute on Violence, Abuse and Trauma (IVAT) in San Diego, CA; and on the Advisory Board of the Clinical Counseling Psychology Review (CCPR) published by the University of Management and Technology, Lahore, Pakistan. She is a member of Zonta International. In her off-time, Pamela spends time with family and friends; paints, sings, reads, travels, and gardens for pleasure; and is involved in various types of physical exercise. She would like her tombstone to read: "She tried her best. She made a difference."

You can learn more about Pam and her work and life through the following sites:

Websites:
https://ivatcenters.org/stop-the-silence
https://www.drpamelajpine.com
https://www.amazon.com/author/pamela.j.pine

Facebook:
https://www.facebook.com/DrPamelaJPine2
https://www.facebook.com/stopcsa
https://www.facebook.com/groups/nikkilove

LinkedIn:
https://www.linkedin.com/in/pamela-j-pine-3123b78/
https://www.linkedin.com/groups/1867777/

Instagram:
pamela.j.pine

Twitter:
@StopSilence_CSA

"Many survivors insist that they're not courageous:
'If I were courageous, I would have stopped the abuse.'
'If I were courageous, I wouldn't be scared.'
Most of us have it mixed up.
You don't start with courage and then face your fear.
You become courageous because you face your fear."

~ Laura Davis, Co-Author (with Ellen Bass), *The Courage to Heal.*

And here I will celebrate this day
Of gain and loss, of darkness, and of beauty and light
Of learning and experience
Of hard work, plenty, and forfeiture
And hold them all together as one

~ Pamela Pine (stanza from a Poem called *"Clocks Forward,"* 2022)